Colorful File Folder Games

Carson-Dellosa Publishing Company, Inc.
Greensboro, North Carolina

Colorful File Folder Games

GRADE 3

Table of Contents

Introduction.. 3-6

Language Arts Games
- Game, Set, Match (identifying antonyms and synonyms) 7-11
- Going Fishing (identifying prefixes, suffixes, and root words)... 12-15
- Treasure Hunt (classifying words)... 16-19
- Under Construction (using words with multiple meanings, using context clues) 20-23
- Busy as a Bee (identifying similes and metaphors) 24-27
- Colorful Words (identifying parts of speech) 28-32
- Presenting Sentences (identifying types of sentences)... 33-36
- Floating Fragments (identifying complete and incomplete sentences) 37-40

Math Games
- Fishing for Facts (multiplication and division facts, multiples) 41-45
- Planting Place Value (identifying place value) 46-50
- Rounding Up Numbers (rounding to nearest ten or hundred)... 51-54
- Making Money (adding and subtracting money) 55-58
- The Big Cheese (adding fractions with common denominators) 59-63
- Measure Up! (customary and metric units of measurement) 64-68
- Guessing Gum Balls (probability) 69-74
- What's Cooking? (making and interpreting a pictograph) 75-80

Credits

Authors: Melissa Hughes, Caroline Lenzo
Editors: Donna Walkush, Caroline Davis, Jennifer Taylor
Layout Design: Mark Conrad
Art Project Coordinator: Julie Kinlaw
Inside Illustrations: Bill Neville
Cover Design: Annette Hollister-Papp
Cover Illustration: J.J. Rudisill
Content Reviewer: Nancy Andrews

© 2006, Carson-Dellosa Publishing Company, Inc., Greensboro, North Carolina 27425. The purchase of this material entitles the buyer to reproduce worksheets and activities for classroom use only—not for commercial resale. Reproduction of these materials for an entire school or district is prohibited. No part of this book may be reproduced (except as noted above), stored in a retrieval system, or transmitted in any form or by any means (mechanically, electronically, recording, etc.) without the prior written consent of Carson-Dellosa Publishing Co., Inc.

Printed in the USA • All rights reserved.

ISBN 1-59441-090-9

Introduction

General Instructions

Materials Needed for Each Game:
- letter-size file folder
- poster board
- resealable plastic bag
- scissors
- glue, rubber cement, or spray adhesive
- lamination film or clear contact paper (optional)

Directions:
1. For each game, remove the game board pages. Glue the pages to a file folder, overlapping them to complete the scene. Note: Due to the printing process, the game board panels may not align precisely. If needed, trim off part of the border.
2. Cut out the game label and glue it to the tab on the file folder.
3. Cut out the game instructions and glue them to the front of the folder.
4. Glue the game cards, game pieces, and answer key to poster board. Then, cut them out.
5. Laminate the game folder, game pieces, and answer key or cover with clear contact paper for durability.
6. On the back of each file folder, attach a resealable plastic bag to make a storage pocket for the game pieces and answer key.

Additional Suggestions:
You may wish to code the game pieces, for example, by writing the game title's initials on the back of each piece. Or, color code each game. For example, glue the game board to a yellow file folder and glue the game cards, game pieces, and answer key to yellow poster board. These methods will quickly identify the game to which a misplaced piece should be returned.

Language Arts Games

Game, Set, Match

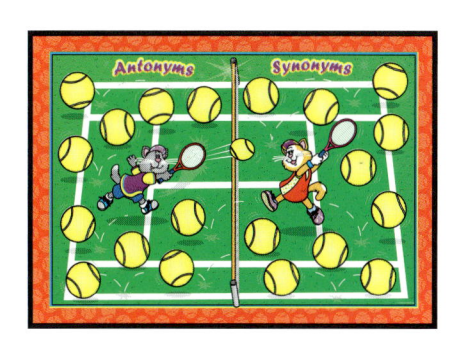

Skills: To match words having similar meanings; to identify synonyms and antonyms; to build vocabulary

Special Instructions:
Write the words on chart paper and have students use them in sentences before playing the game.

Going Fishing

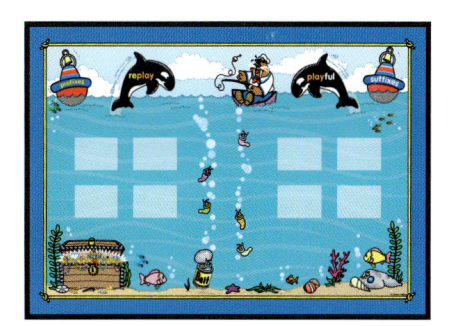

Skills: To identify common prefixes and suffixes; to identify root words

Treasure Hunt

Skill: To classify words by categories

Under Construction

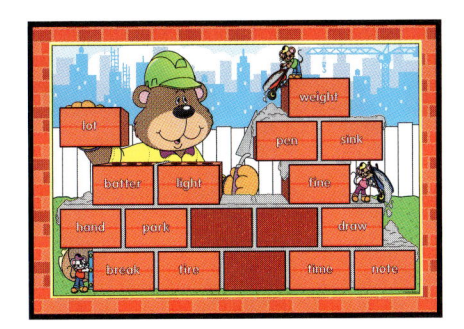

Skills: To identify the best word that completes a sentence; to demonstrate knowledge of words with multiple meanings

Busy as a Bee

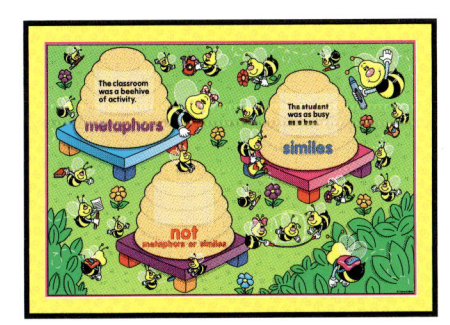

Skill: To identify similes and metaphors in context

Colorful Words

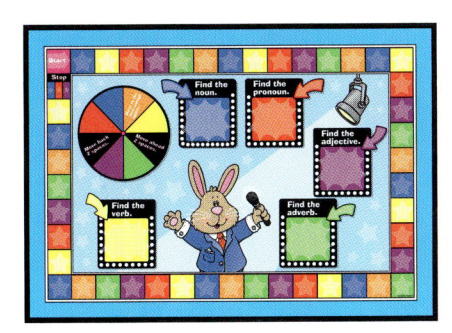

Skill: To identify parts of speech by using sentence context

Colorful Words, continued

Special Instructions:
Include a large paper clip and a pencil with the game pieces. To use the spinner, instruct students to place one end of the paper clip over the center of the spinner area. Then, have them place the tip of the pencil through the paper clip so that it touches the center of the spinner. The paper clip will rotate around the pencil when a student spins the paper clip.

To make the game markers, cut out the pieces and then fold each one on the dashed lines to make a tent-shaped game marker.

Before students play the game, determine which parts of speech they can identify. Remove cards that contain parts of speech that they cannot identify. If not all of the cards are used and a student spins that particular color, she may move her game marker to the nearest space on the game board without providing an answer.

Presenting Sentences

Skill: To identify types of sentences

© Carson-Dellosa — CD-104051 *Colorful File Folder Games*

Floating Fragments

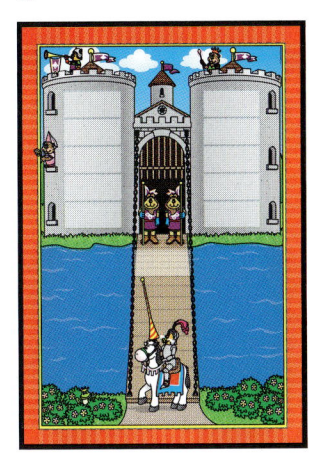

Skills: To identify complete sentences and fragments

Math Games

Fishing for Facts

Skills: To demonstrate knowledge of multiplication and division facts; to identify multiples of 3-9

Planting Place Value

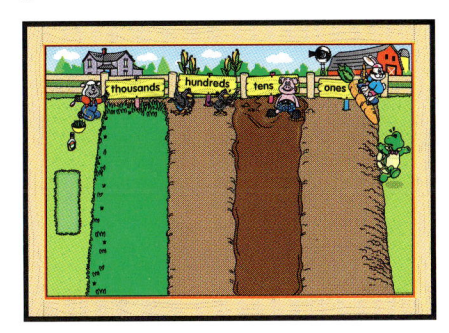

Skills: To identify the place value of digits within numbers up to 9,999; to match standard numbers to expanded numbers

Rounding Up Numbers

Skills: To round numbers to nearest 10; to round numbers to nearest 100

Making Money

Skills: To add and subtract money

Special Instructions:
To extend the game, have students start with $40.00 or more in their banks and place all of the cards facedown in a stack on the game board. Have students take turns drawing cards to fill the spaces on their banks and determining their new totals.

© Carson-Dellosa

CD-104051 *Colorful File Folder Games*

The Big Cheese

Skills: To add fractions with common denominators (halves, thirds, fourths, sixths); to add fractional parts to get whole numbers

Special Instructions:
To make the game markers, cut out the pieces and then fold each one on the dashed lines to make a tent-shaped game marker.

Measure Up!

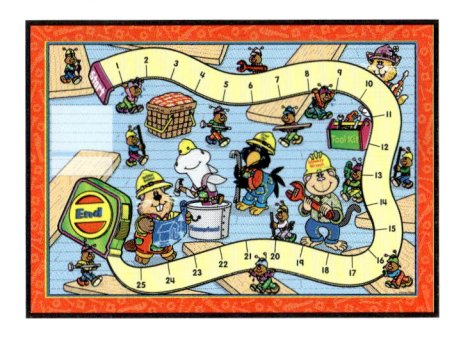

Skill: To select the appropriate unit of measurement (customary or metric) for length, weight, or capacity of objects

Special Instructions:
To make the game markers, cut out the pieces and then fold each one on the dashed lines to make a tent-shaped game marker.

Guessing Gum Balls

Skill: To use data to describe probability of events

What's Cooking?

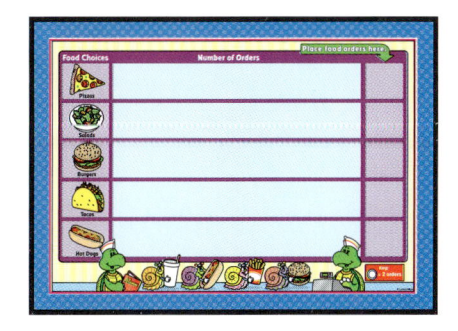

Skills: To collect and organize data; to interpret a pictograph

Game, Set, Match

Game, Set, Match

Directions

1. Take the game cards and answer key out of the pocket. Turn the answer key facedown.
2. Arrange the cards facedown in five rows with eight cards in a row.
3. Choose two cards and turn them faceup. If the words are antonyms, place both game pieces on a tennis ball on the Antonyms side of the game board.
4. If the words are synonyms, place both game pieces on a tennis ball on the Synonyms side of the game board.
5. If the words are not antonyms or synonyms, place both cards facedown in their original positions.
6. Continue playing until all of the words have been matched and placed on the game board.
7. Use the answer key to check your work.

Game, Set, Match
Answer Key

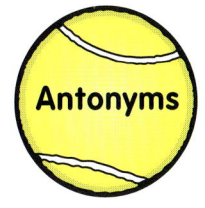

Antonyms
- arrive—leave
- awake—asleep
- begin—end
- cheap—expensive
- clean—filthy
- forget—remember
- lead—follow
- noisy—silent
- raise—lower
- silly—serious

Synonyms
- answer—respond
- brave—heroic
- center—middle
- choose—select
- damp—moist
- harm—injure
- quick—rapid
- shy—timid
- small—tiny
- strange—unusual

Synonyms

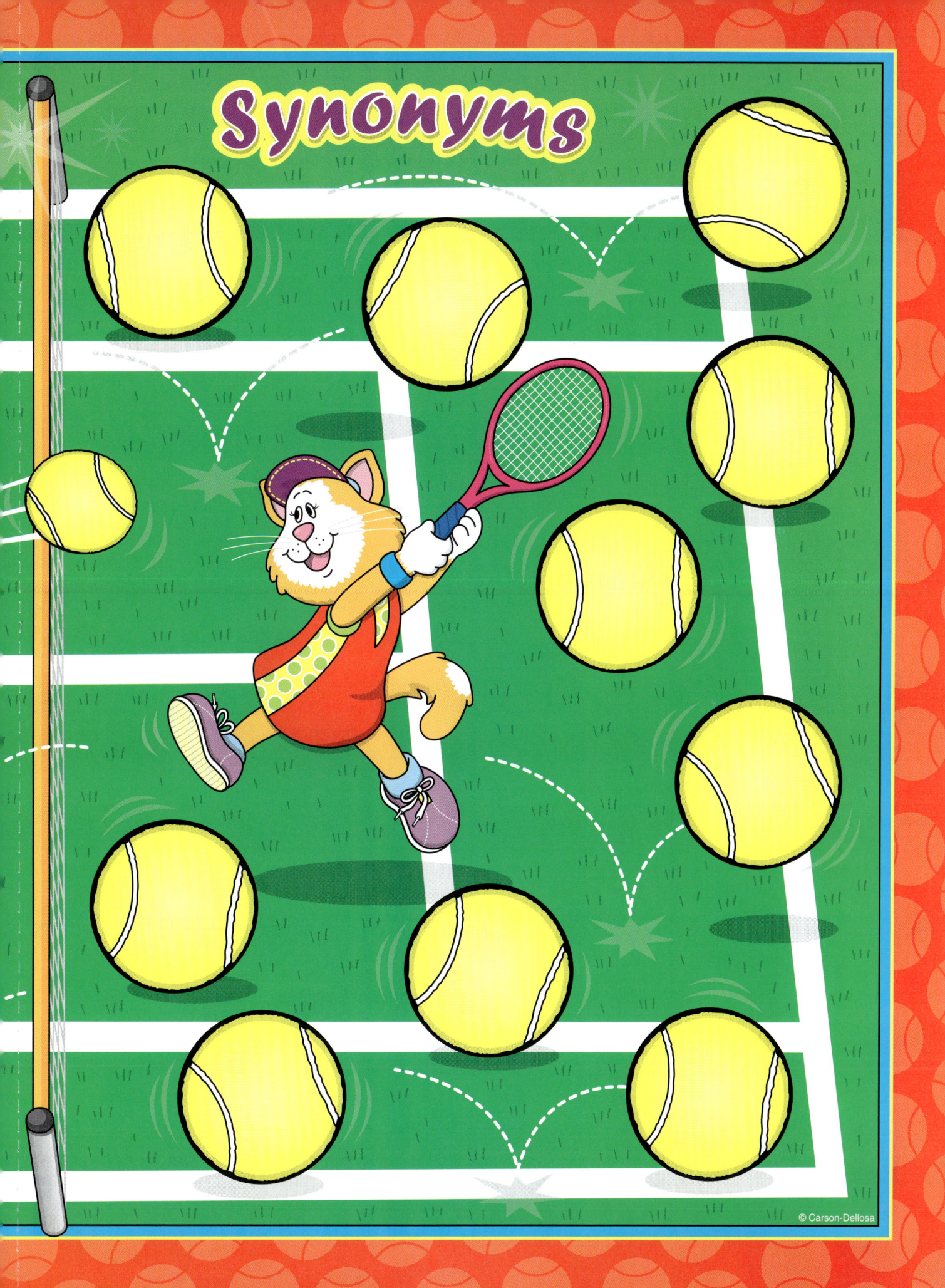

Antonyms

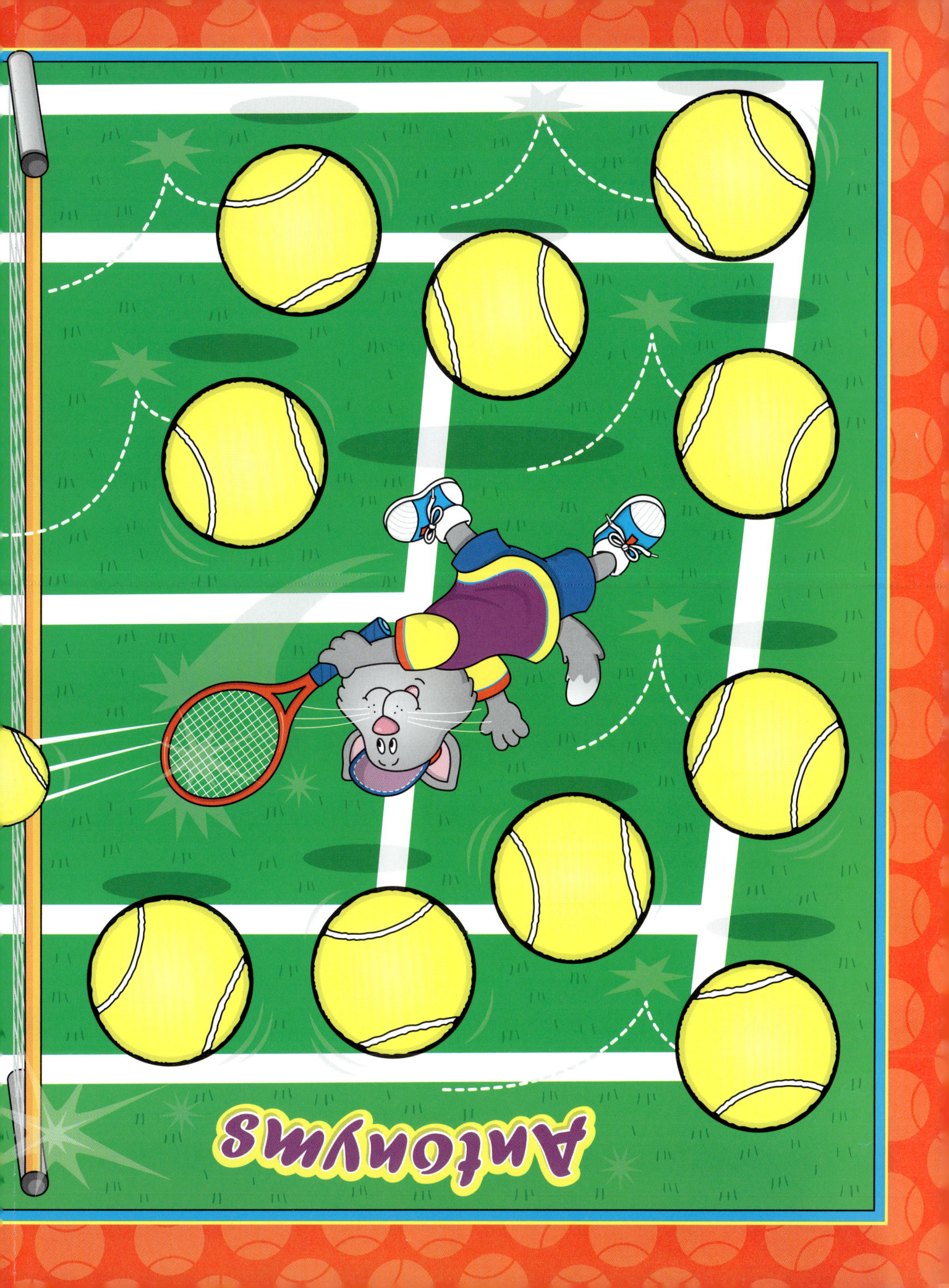

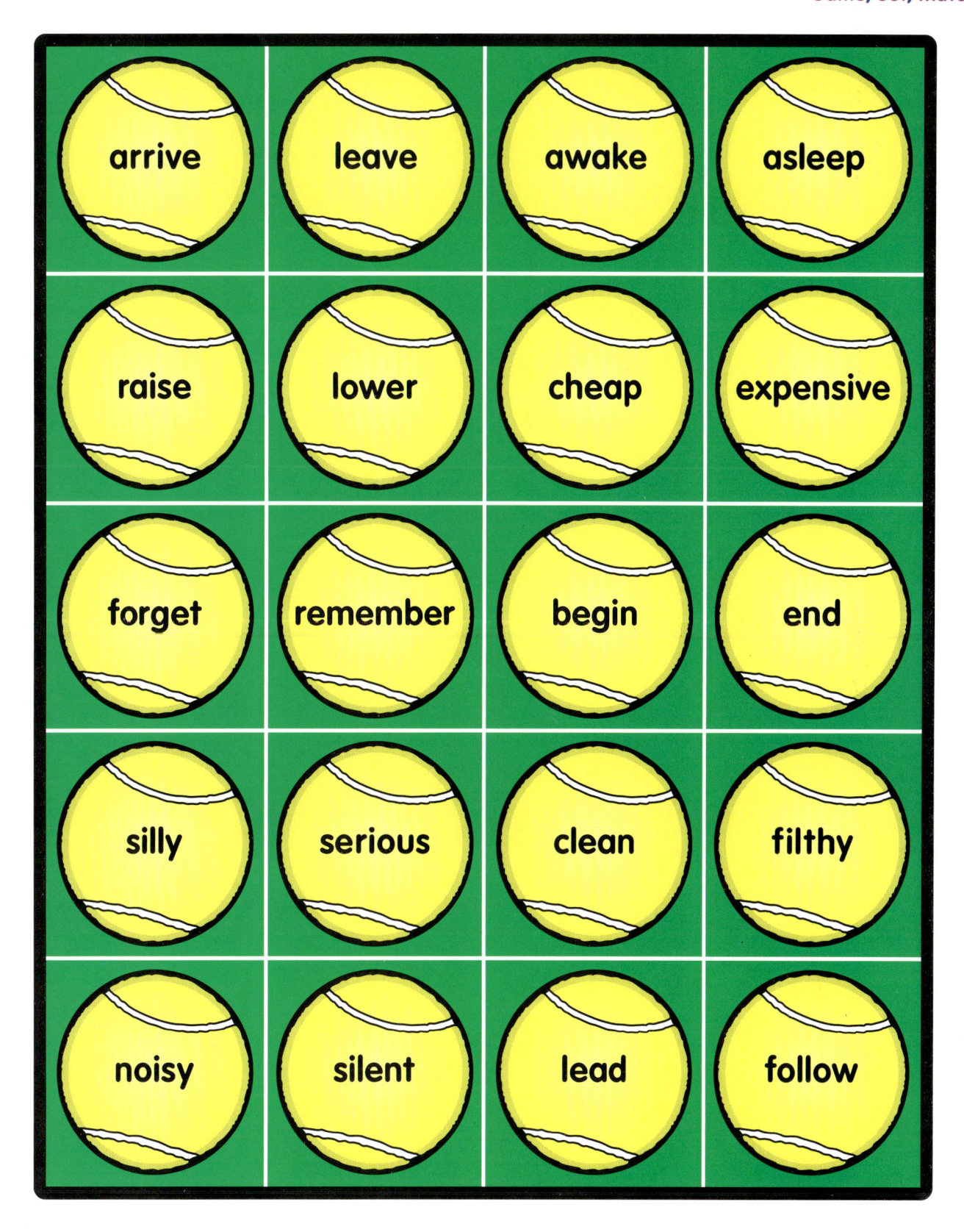

Game, Set, Match

arrive	leave	awake	asleep
raise	lower	cheap	expensive
forget	remember	begin	end
silly	serious	clean	filthy
noisy	silent	lead	follow

Game, Set, Match

center	middle	damp	moist
answer	respond	strange	unusual
quick	rapid	shy	timid
choose	select	small	tiny
harm	injure	brave	heroic

Going Fishing

Directions

1. Ask a friend to play the game with you.
2. Take the game cards and answer key out of the pocket. Turn the answer key facedown.
3. Shuffle the game cards, then give each player four cards. Place the other cards facedown in a stack near the game board.
4. Have each player sort his cards into two groups, one for prefixes and one for suffixes.
5. Choose a prefix or suffix, then try to get four cards with matching prefixes or suffixes. To do this, take turns fishing for cards by asking Player 2 if he has a card with the prefix or suffix you need.
6. If Player 2 has a card that you ask for, he should give you the card. If he does not have a card, choose a card from the stack of cards on the game board.
7. When a player finds four cards with the same prefix or suffix, he should place the four cards in a box on the correct side of the game board.
8. Continue playing until all boxes on the game board are filled.
9. Use the answer key to check your work.

Going Fishing
Answer Key

prefixes

disagree	reappear
disappear	rejoin
dislike	reread
disobey	rewind

misbehave	unkind
miscount	unreal
mislead	unwind
misspell	unwrap

suffixes

dancer	careful
leader	colorful
runner	helpful
teacher	wonderful

cleanest	endless
darkest	helpless
softest	hopeless
thinnest	sugarless

© Carson-Dellosa — CD-104051 Colorful File Folder Games

playful

suffixes

replay

prefixes

Going Fishing

endless	helpless	hopeless	sugarless
helpful	careful	wonderful	colorful
cleanest	darkest	softest	thinnest
dancer	leader	runner	teacher
unkind	unreal	unwind	unwrap
reappear	rejoin	reread	rewind
misbehave	miscount	mislead	misspell
disagree	disappear	dislike	disobey

Treasure Hunt

Treasure Hunt

Directions

Game 1

1. Take the jewels and answer key out of the pocket. Turn the answer key facedown.
2. Put a yellow category jewel on the front of each treasure chest.
3. Scatter the other jewels faceup around the game board.
4. Sort the jewels by category, then place them inside the treasure chests with the correct category label.
5. Continue playing until all of the jewels have been sorted.
6. Use the answer key to check your work.

Game 2

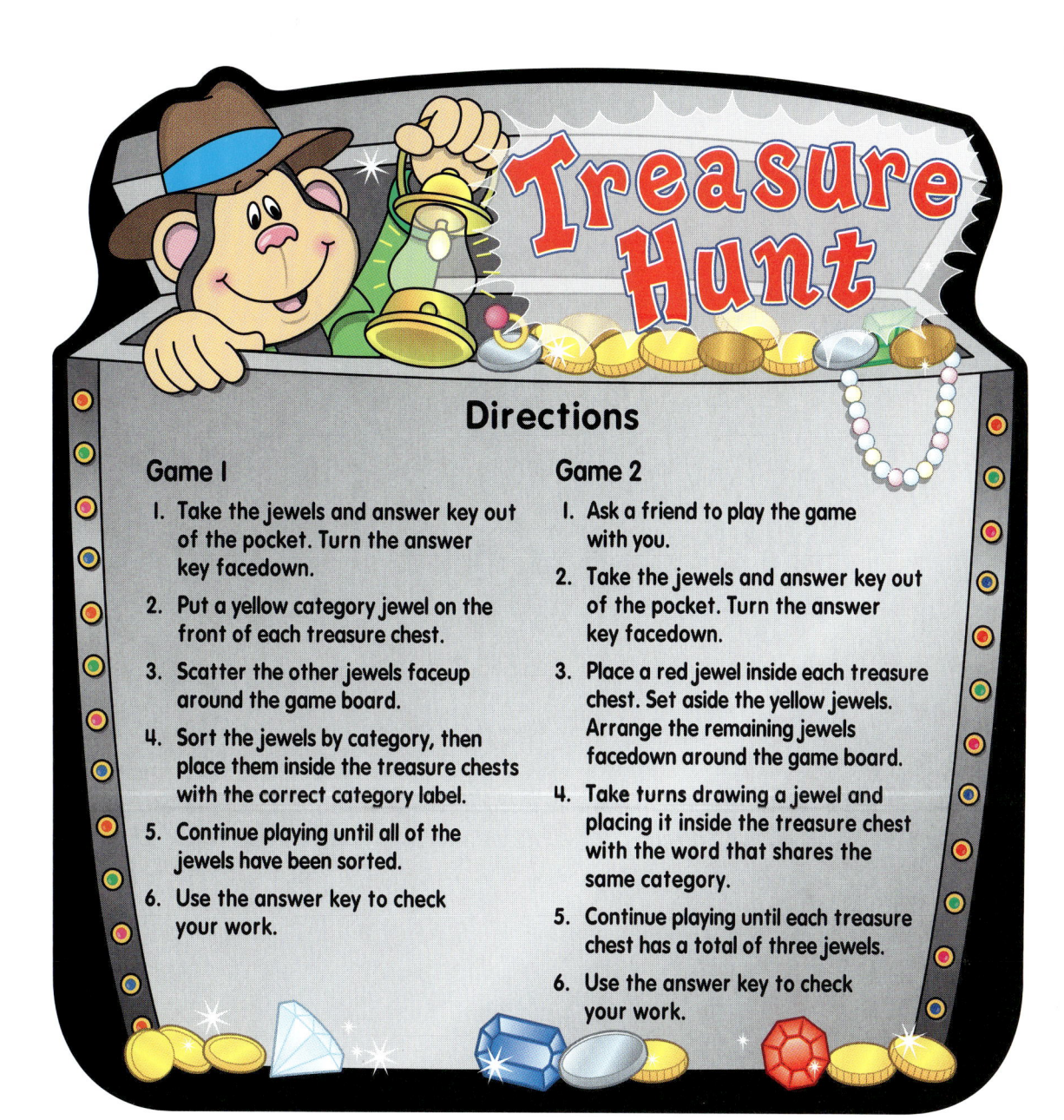

1. Ask a friend to play the game with you.
2. Take the jewels and answer key out of the pocket. Turn the answer key facedown.
3. Place a red jewel inside each treasure chest. Set aside the yellow jewels. Arrange the remaining jewels facedown around the game board.
4. Take turns drawing a jewel and placing it inside the treasure chest with the word that shares the same category.
5. Continue playing until each treasure chest has a total of three jewels.
6. Use the answer key to check your work.

Treasure Hunt
Answer Key

Animals
crocodile
elephant
shark

Foods
apple
macaroni
watermelon

Sounds
buzz
squeal
whimper

Transportation
airplane
automobile
motorcycle

Emotions
excited
angry
scared

Land Formations
mountain
plain
valley

Space
comets
planets
stars

Weather
lightning
raindrops
sleet

© Carson-Dellosa　　　CD-104051 *Colorful File Folder Games*

© Carson-Dellosa

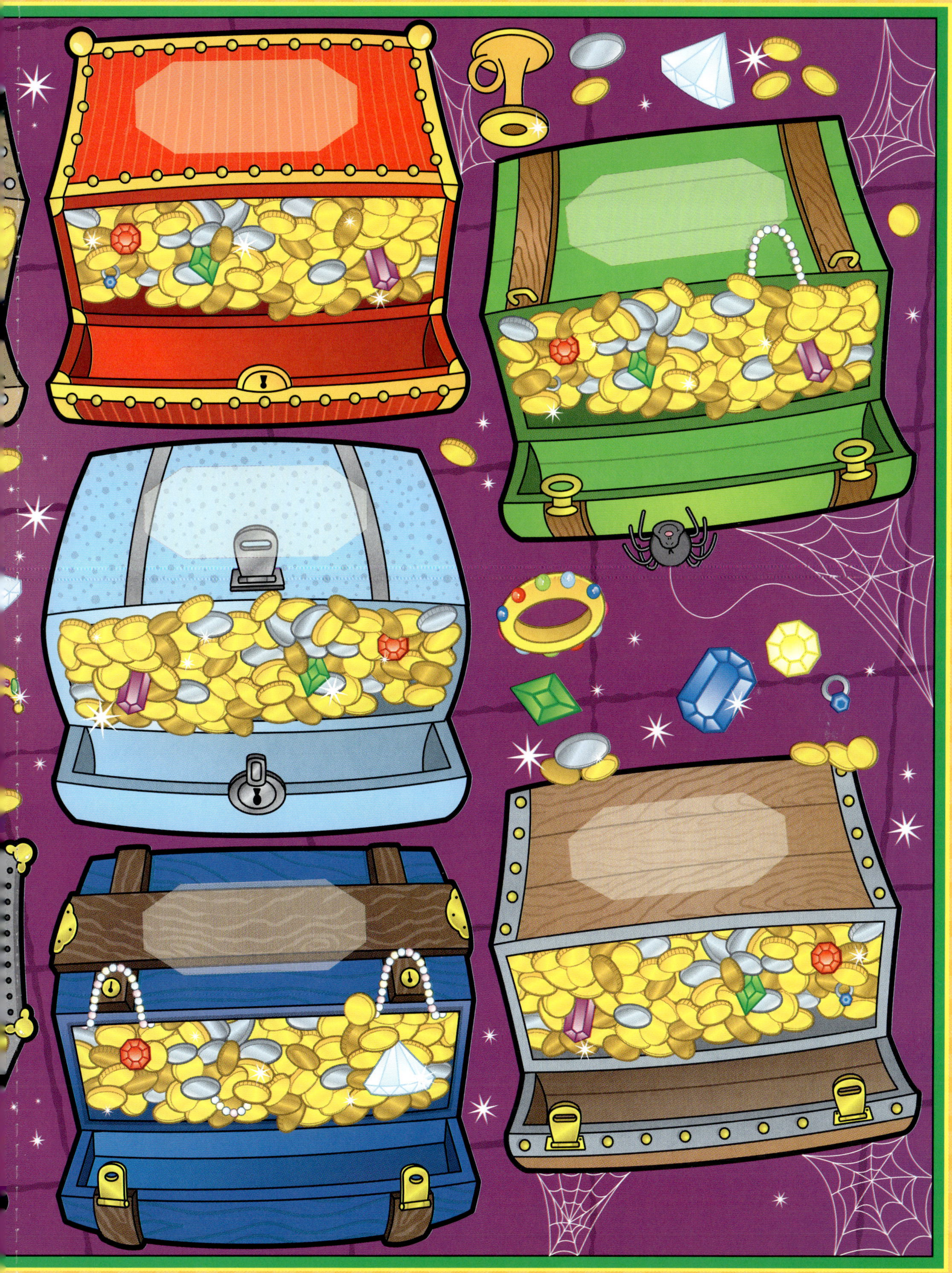

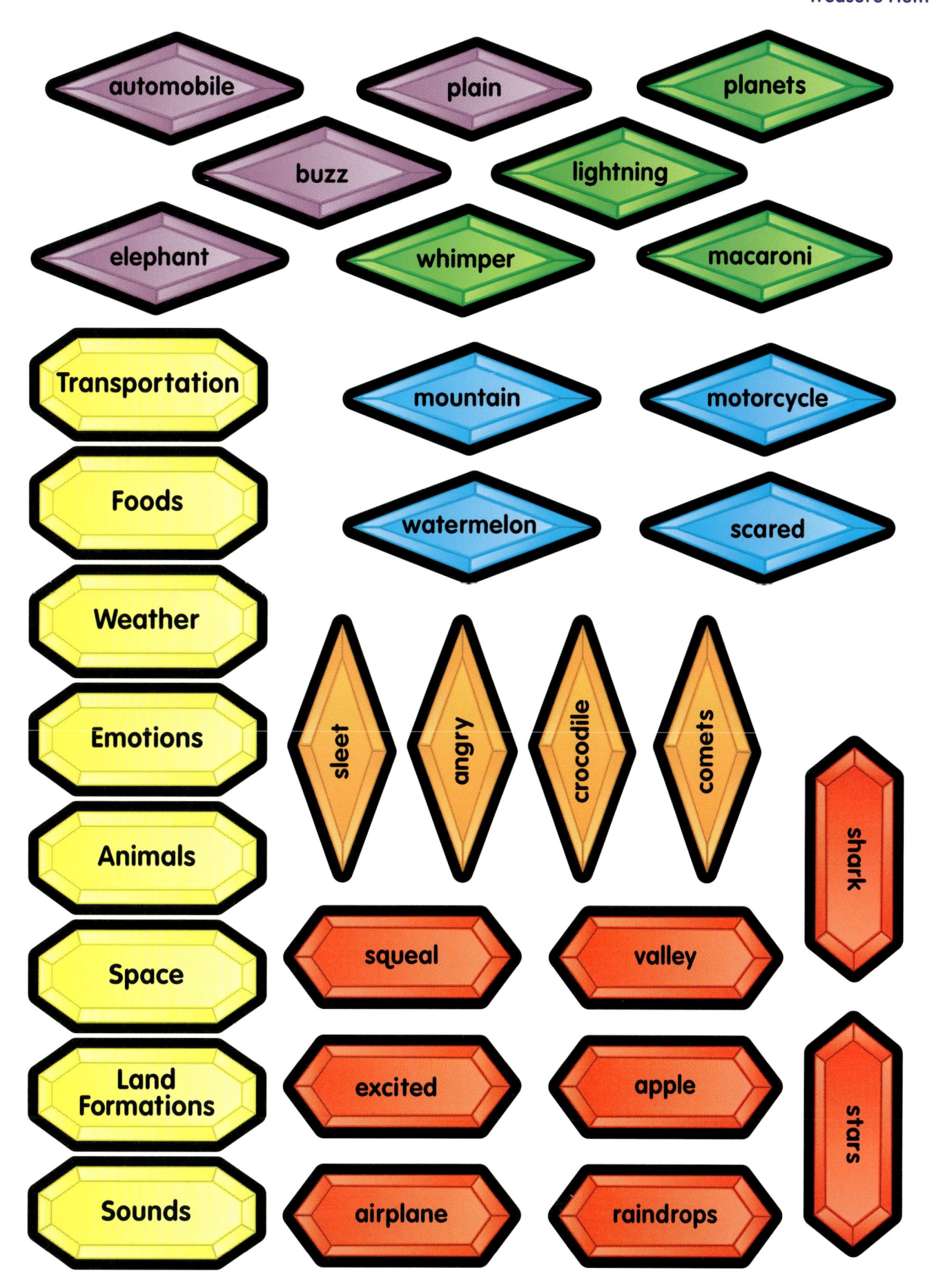

Treasure Hunt

- automobile
- plain
- planets
- buzz
- lightning
- elephant
- whimper
- macaroni
- mountain
- motorcycle
- watermelon
- scared
- sleet
- angry
- crocodile
- comets
- shark
- squeal
- valley
- excited
- apple
- stars
- airplane
- raindrops

Categories:
- Transportation
- Foods
- Weather
- Emotions
- Animals
- Space
- Land Formations
- Sounds

# Under Construction

Directions

1. Ask a friend to play the game with you.
2. Take the game cards and answer key out of the pocket. Turn the answer key facedown. Place the game cards faceup in a pile near the game board.
3. Have each player choose one side of the game board.
4. Take turns choosing a card and reading the sentence. Find the word on the game board that completes the sentence. If the word is on your side of the game board, place the game card on the word. If the word is not on your side of the game board, place the game card at the bottom of the stack.
5. The first player to cover each word on her side of the game board with two game cards is the winner.
6. Use the answer key to check your work.

Under Construction
Answer Key

Chen and his friends cleaned up the empty lot on the corner.
Jean paid a lot of money for her new car.

Elizabeth was the first batter to hit a home run.
Keisha helped her mother make the pancake batter.

Gabe turned on the light so that he could see to read.
It is cool enough to wear a light jacket.

Please hand me that paper.
Ramiro couldn't go swimming because he broke his hand.

Please park the car in the driveway.
It was a beautiful day to spend some time at the park.

Let's work hard until noon and then take a break.
Be careful not to break the glass bowl.

By the end of the game, the players were beginning to tire.
Olivia couldn't ride her bike because it had a flat tire.

Jena measured the weight of the box on the scale.
Sarah added another weight to the barbell.

The sheep got out of their pen and were wandering around the fields.
My pen broke, and the ink stained my shirt.

Please put your dinner dishes in the sink.
The heavy box began to sink slowly to the bottom of the lake.

The students did a fine job on the project.
Tyler had to pay a fine for his overdue library books.

If you draw the curtains, the sun won't shine in your eyes.
Carlos likes to draw and paint pictures of horses.

Emily wrote a note telling her mother what time she would be home.
The singer hit the high note beautifully.

What time do you have to be at school?
Jamal used a stopwatch to time Amber running the 50-yard dash.

© Carson-Dellosa … CD-104051 *Colorful File Folder Games*

weight

pen

sink

fine

draw

time

note

tire

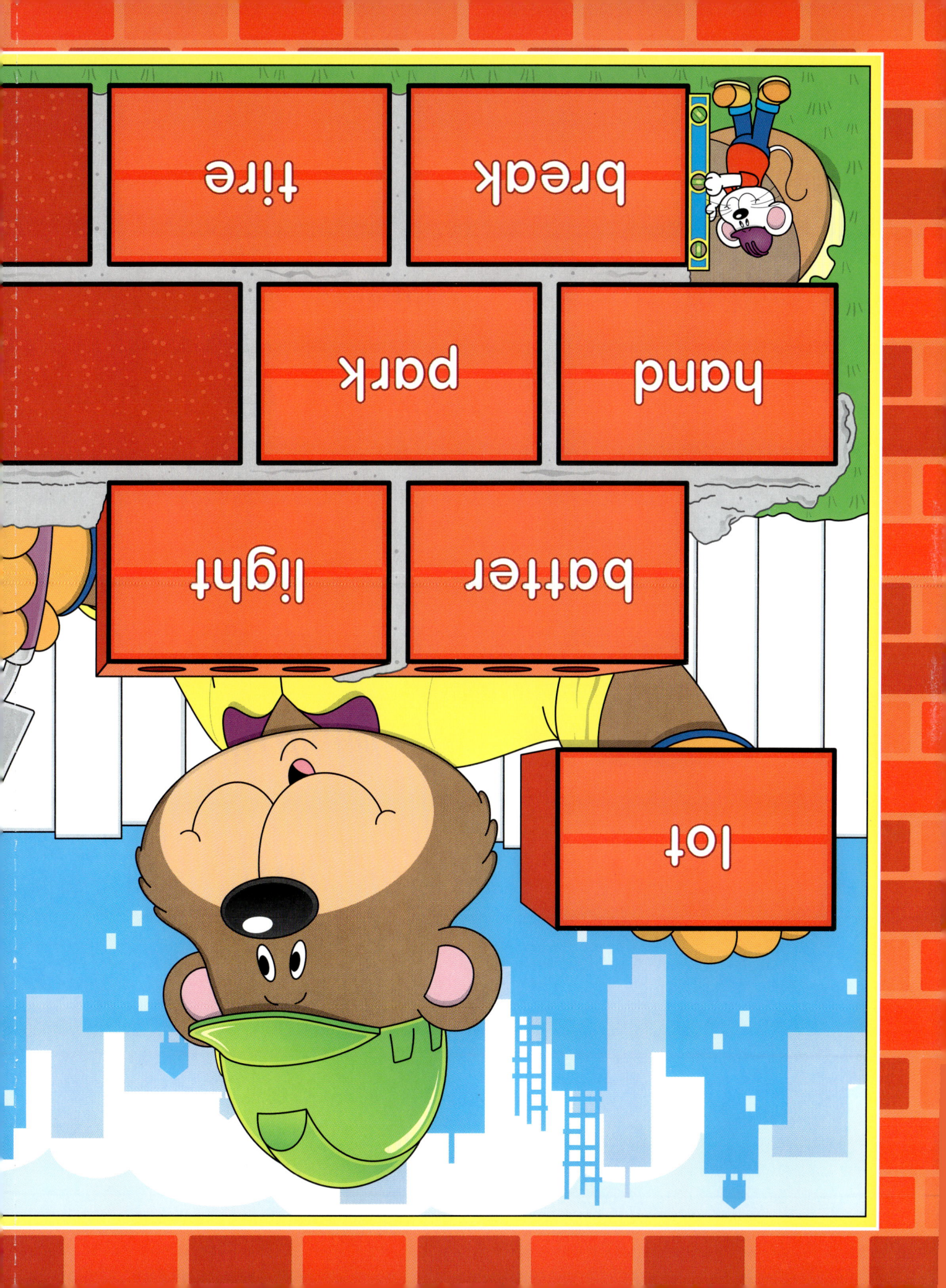

break

park

hand

light

batter

lot

Under Construction

Keisha helped her mother make the pancake _____.	Elizabeth was the first _____ to hit a home run.	Jean paid a _____ of money for her new car.	Chen and his friends cleaned up the empty _____ on the corner.
Ramiro couldn't go swimming because he broke his _____.	Please _____ me that paper.	It is cool enough to wear a _____ jacket.	Gabe turned on the _____ so that he could see to read.
Be careful not to _____ the glass bowl.	Let's work hard until noon and then take a _____.	It was a beautiful day to spend some time at the _____.	Please _____ the car in the driveway.
Tyler had to pay a _____ for his overdue library books.	The students did a _____ job on the project.	Olivia couldn't ride her bike because it had a flat _____.	By the end of the game, the players were beginning to _____.
My _____ broke, and the ink stained my shirt.	The sheep got out of their _____ and were wandering around the fields.	Sarah added another _____ to the barbell.	Jena measured the _____ of the box on the scale.
Carlos likes to _____ and paint pictures of horses.	If you _____ the curtains, the sun won't shine in your eyes.	The heavy box began to _____ slowly to the bottom of the lake.	Please put your dinner dishes in the _____.
Jamal used a stopwatch to _____ Amber running the 50-yard dash.	What _____ do you have to be at school?	The singer hit the high _____ beautifully.	Emily wrote a _____ telling her mother what time she would be home.

© Carson-Dellosa 23 CD-104051 *Colorful File Folder Games*

Busy as a Bee

Directions

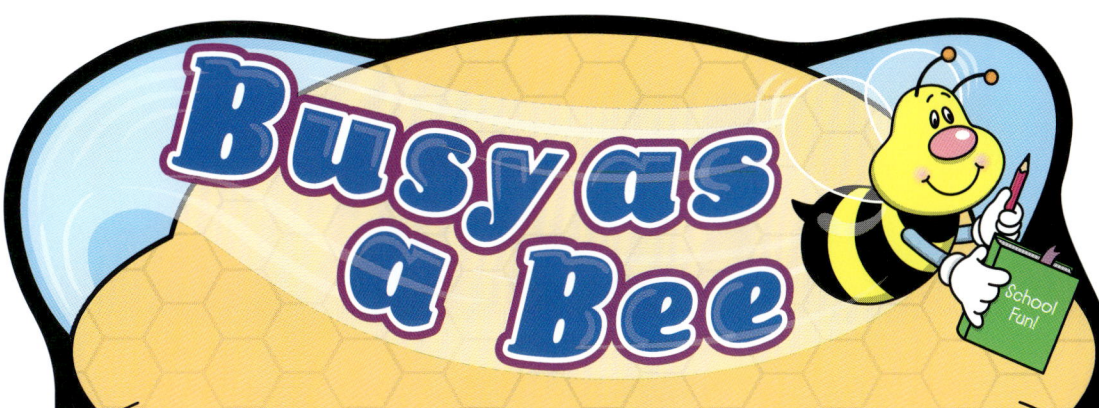

1. Take the game cards and answer key out of the pocket. Turn the answer key facedown.

2. Place the game cards faceup in a pile near the game board.

3. Choose a game card and read the sentence. Decide if the sentence is an example of a metaphor or simile. Then, place the game card on the correct beehive.

4. If the sentence is not an example of a metaphor or simile, place it on the Not Metaphors or Similes beehive.

5. Use the answer key to check your work.

Busy as a Bee
Answer Key

Metaphors
Carmen was a machine cleaning the house before the party.

The grass was a plush, green carpet for our bare feet.

The calm lake was a mirror reflecting the sky.

The leaves were dancers on the breeze.

The clouds were white puffs of cotton.

The ice cream shop had a rainbow of flavors.

Similes
Kayla was as quiet as a mouse.

The snow covered the ground like a soft, white blanket.

The old bed was as hard as a rock.

The car engine roared like a freight train.

Jim's feet were as cold as ice.

The dew sparkled like diamonds in the sunlight.

Not Metaphors or Similes
Tomas raked the leaves into piles.

The dancers leaped across the stage.

The duck paddled in the pond.

Ariel bounced on the bed.

Fiona mowed the lawn yesterday.

The tiny mouse scurried to its nest.

The student was as busy as a bee.

similes

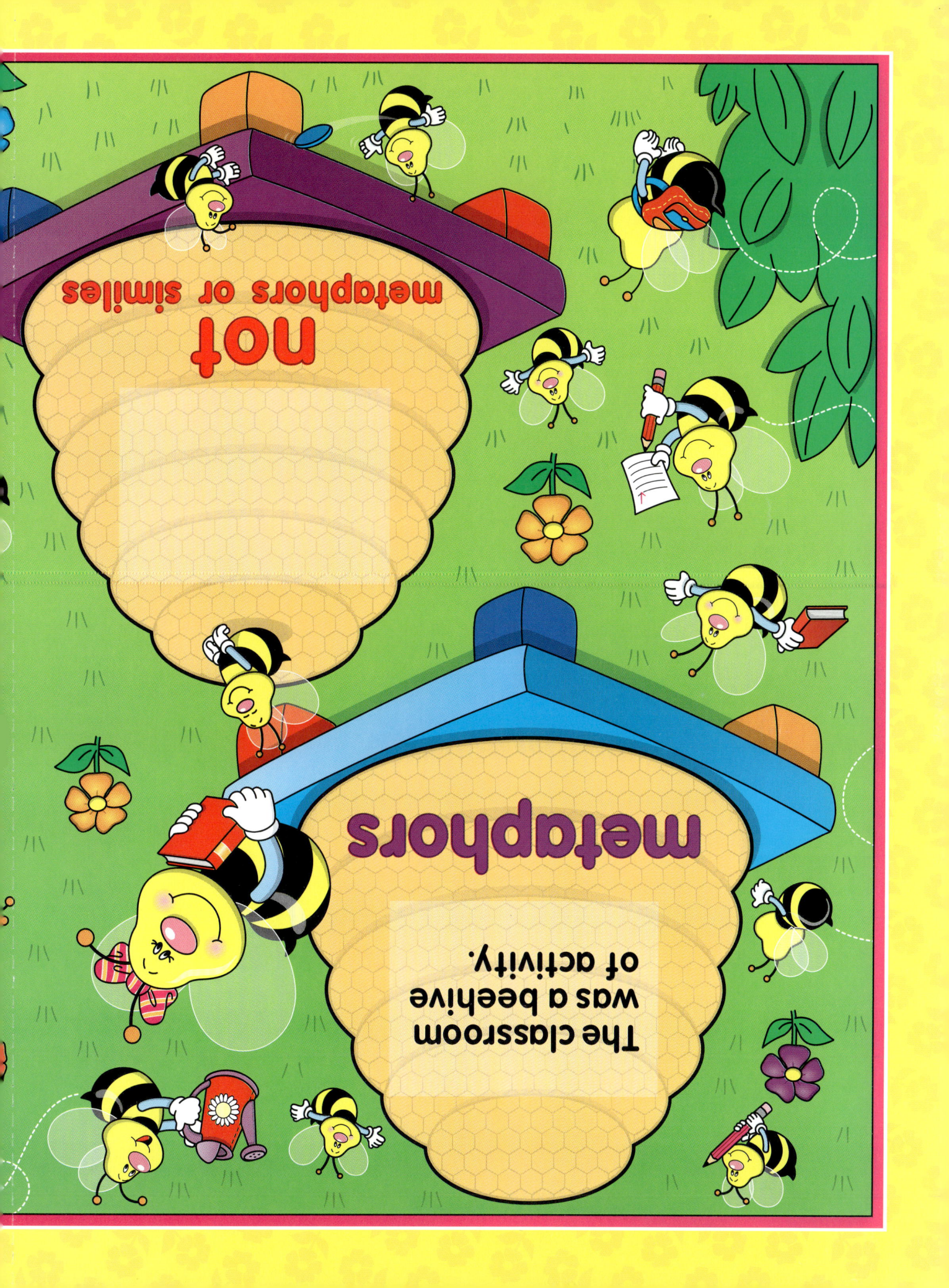

metaphors

The classroom was a beehive of activity.

not metaphors or similes

Busy as a Bee

Kayla was as quiet as a mouse.	The snow covered the ground like a soft, white blanket.	The old bed was as hard as a rock.
The car engine roared like a freight train.	Jim's feet were as cold as ice.	The dew sparkled like diamonds in the sunlight.
Carmen was a machine cleaning the house before the party.	The grass was a plush, green carpet for our bare feet.	The calm lake was a mirror reflecting the sky.
The leaves were dancers on the breeze.	The clouds were white puffs of cotton.	The ice cream shop had a rainbow of flavors.
Tomas raked the leaves into piles.	The dancers leaped across the stage.	The duck paddled in the pond.
Ariel bounced on the bed.	Fiona mowed the lawn yesterday.	The tiny mouse scurried to its nest.

© Carson-Dellosa   27   CD-104051 *Colorful File Folder Games*

Colorful Words

Directions

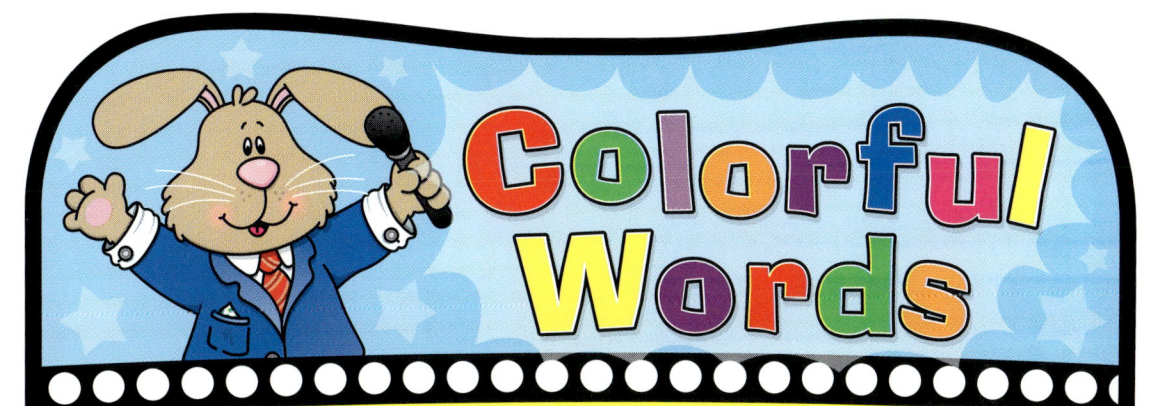

1. Ask a friend to play the game with you.

2. Take the game cards, game markers, and answer key out of the pocket. Turn the answer key facedown.

3. Sort the cards by colors. Shuffle each set of cards and place them facedown in a stack on the game board on the correct color.

4. Take turns spinning the paper clip spinner and following the directions. If the spinner lands on a color, draw a card from that color stack. Read the sentence aloud and identify the noun, pronoun, adjective, verb, or adverb. Have Player 2 check your answer. If the answer is correct, move your game marker to the next space on the game board that has that color. If the spinner lands on words, follow the directions.

5. The first player to reach "Stop" is the winner.

Colorful Words
Answer Key

Find the noun.	Find the pronoun.	Find the adjective.	Find the verb.	Find the adverb.
1 necklace	9 I	17 wooden	25 ran	33 carefully
2 question	10 She	18 Colorful	26 jumped	34 quickly
3 package	11 He	19 basketball	27 washes	35 loudly
4 dolphin	12 We	20 funny	28 flew	36 happily
5 shoes	13 My	21 fierce	29 skated	37 fast
6 pillow	14 their	22 green	30 hid	38 soundly
7 coin	15 You	23 shy	31 painted	39 softly
8 party	16 her	24 large	32 writes	40 quietly

© Carson-Dellosa   28   CD-104051 *Colorful File Folder Games*

Find the pronoun.

Find the adjective.

Find the adverb.

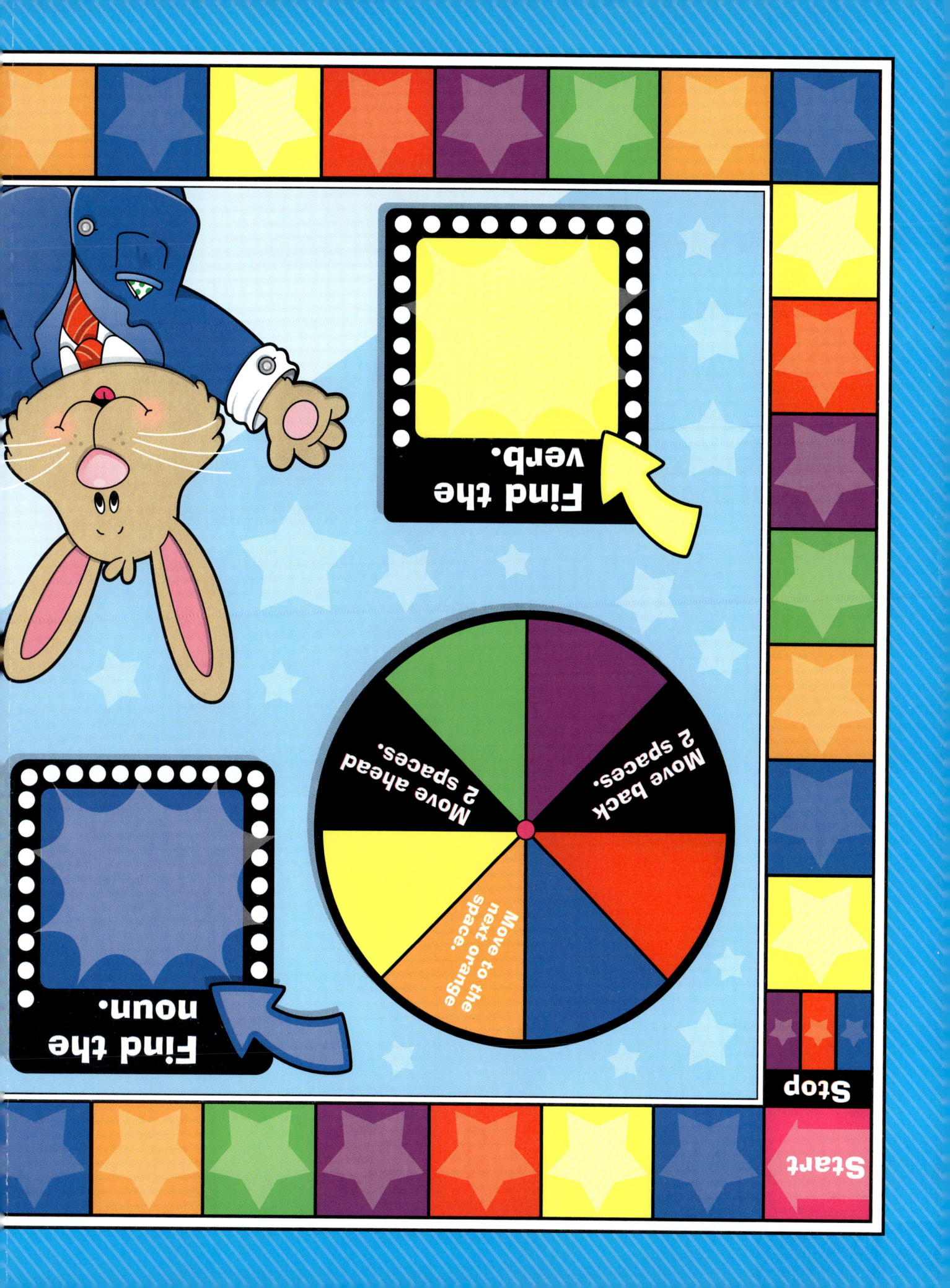

Find the verb.

Find the noun.

Move back 2 spaces.

Move ahead 2 spaces.

Move to the next orange space.

Stop

Start

Colorful Words

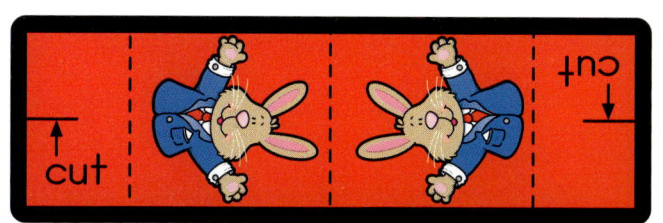

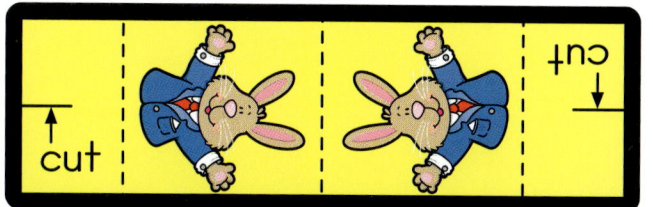

1. The necklace was broken.	2. Answer each question.	3. Please deliver the package.	4. The dolphin splashed wildly.
5. Your new shoes look cool.	6. This large pillow is too soft.	7. This is an old, rare coin.	8. The birthday party was fun.
25. Sakari ran to the neighbor's house.	26. The dog jumped onto the couch.	27. Jamal washes the car on Saturday.	28. The hawk flew high above the trees.
29. Bob skated across the ice rink.	30. Jenny hid the present under the bed.	31. Dylan painted a large picture on the wall.	32. Evita writes a letter to her friend.
9. I like chocolate ice cream the best.	10. She studied the spelling words for 30 minutes.	11. He locked the keys in the car.	12. We want to take a family vacation this summer.

Colorful Words

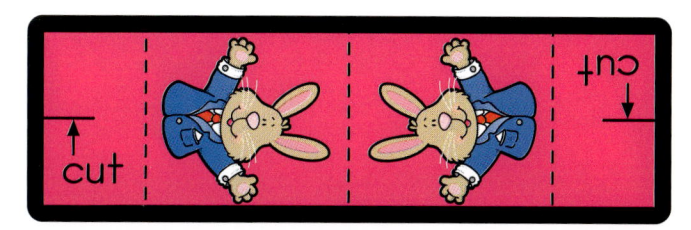

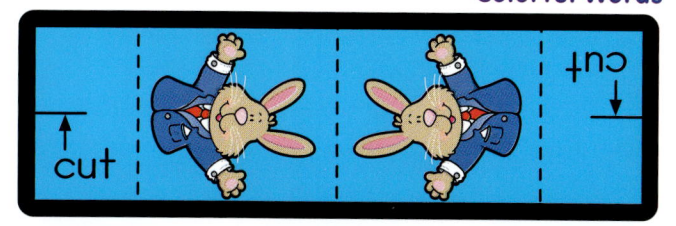

17 The man sat on a wooden bench.	18 Colorful flowers were growing in the garden.	19 The basketball team plays well together.	20 Zoe read a funny book in school.
21 The fierce dog scared the children.	22 I like green apples the best.	23 The shy girl hid behind the tree.	24 Zach built a large fort in the backyard.
33 The boy read the directions carefully.	34 The players ran quickly after the soccer ball.	35 The dog barked loudly.	36 Kara happily opened her gifts.
37 The car moved fast around the racetrack.	38 The child slept soundly in his bed.	39 The librarian spoke softly to the people.	40 The students sat quietly in their seats.
13 My puppy is learning new tricks.	14 The Fleming family invited many people to their party.	15 You did a good job cleaning the room.	16 Patty bought a gift for her grandmother.

Presenting Sentences

Directions

1. Take the game cards and answer key out of the pocket. Turn the answer key facedown.
2. Scatter the blue and yellow cards faceup around the game board.
3. Choose a game card and read the sentence. Decide what type of sentence is shown on the game card. Then, place the game card on the correct space on the game board.
4. Continue playing until all of the game cards are sorted.
5. Use the answer key to check your work.

Presenting Sentences
Answer Key

Questions

Who is coming to the party?
When are we going on vacation?
How many puppies did your dog have?
What time does the bus come?
How fast can you run?
Which movie would you like to see?

Statements

The dog chased the cat into the yard.
Jody rode her bicycle to school.
My friend moved to New York.
My sister was sick last week.
Craig ripped his jeans when he fell.
The cat likes to sit in the sun.

Commands

Put the books on the bottom shelf.
Walk quickly and quietly to the nearest exit.
Put the chess game on the shelf.
Sharpen your pencil before the bell rings.
Help your sister wash the dishes.
Turn off those lights.

Exclamations

What a rainy day!
I love ice cream!
Rosita fell off her bike!
My tooth hurts!
I'm going to be late for school!
I can't wait until summer vacation!

command	question	statement
command	exclamation	question

exclamation	exclamation
statement	command
command	question

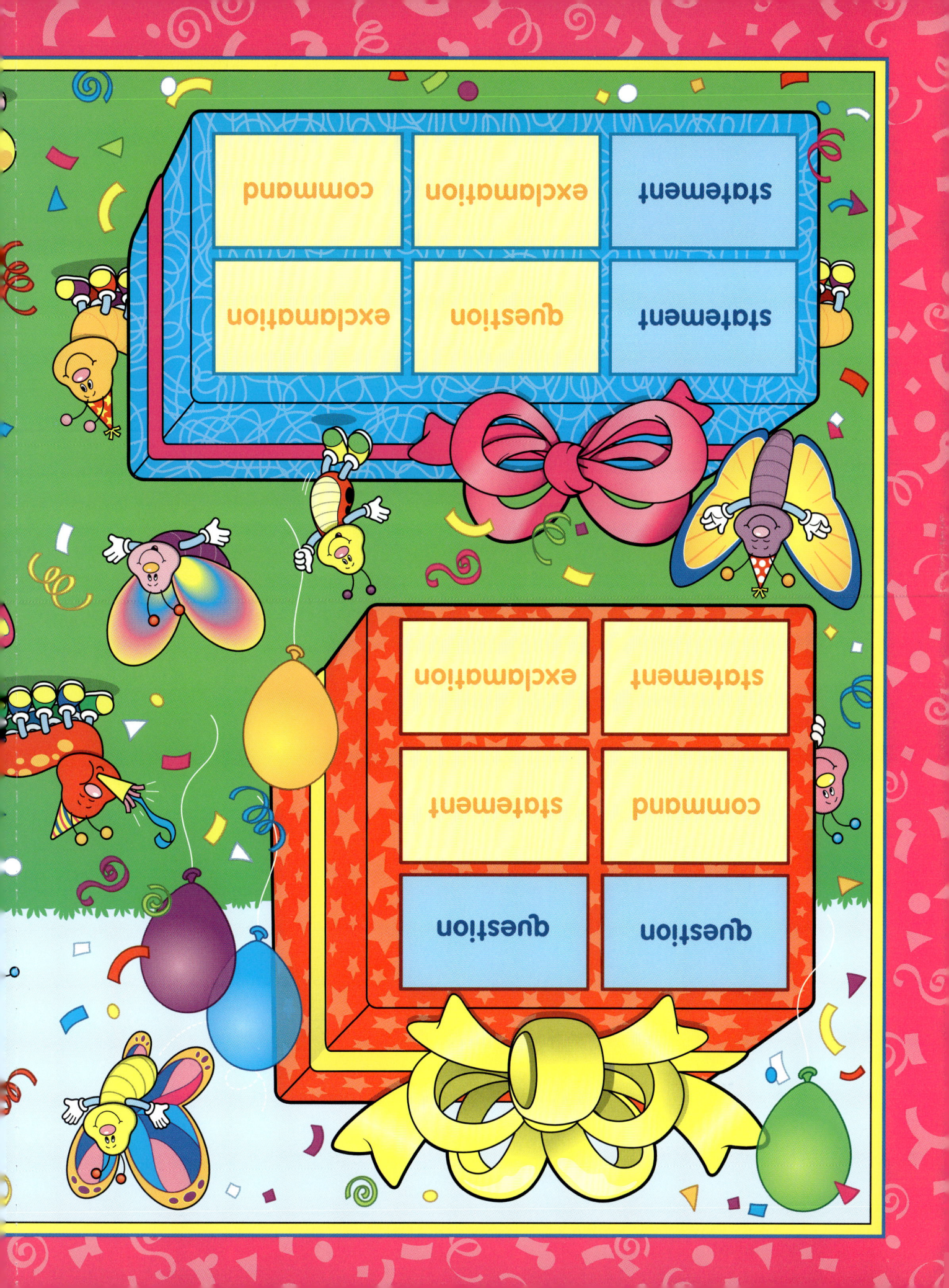

command	exclamation	statement
exclamation	question	statement

exclamation	statement
statement	command
question	question

Presenting Sentences

The dog chased the cat into the yard.	Jody rode her bicycle to school.	Who is coming to the party?	When are we going on vacation?
Put the books on the bottom shelf.	Walk quickly and quietly to the nearest exit.	What a rainy day!	I love ice cream!
My friend moved to New York.	My sister was sick last week.	Craig ripped his jeans when he fell.	The cat likes to sit in the sun.
Rosita fell off her bike!	My tooth hurts!	I'm going to be late for school!	I can't wait until summer vacation!
How many puppies did your dog have?	What time does the bus come?	How fast can you run?	Which movie would you like to see?
Put the chess game on the shelf.	Sharpen your pencil before the bell rings.	Help your sister wash the dishes.	Turn off those lights.

Floating Fragments

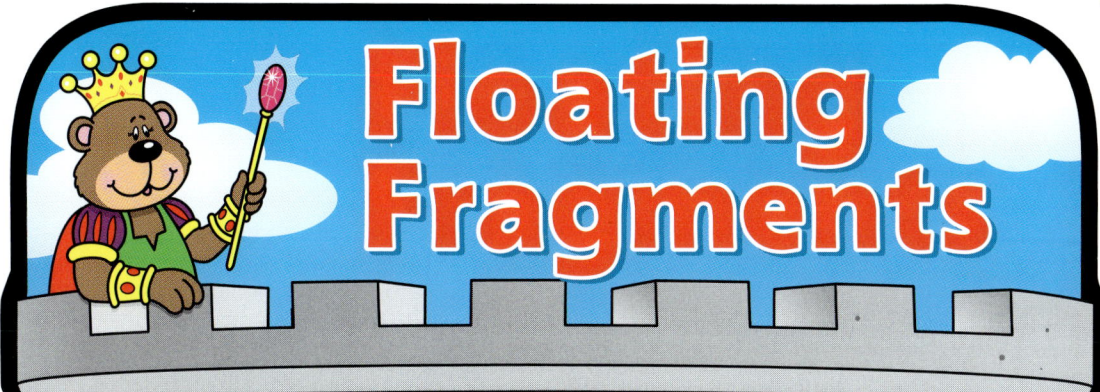

Directions

1. Ask a friend to play the game with you.
2. Take the game cards and answer key out of the pocket. Turn the answer key facedown.
3. Shuffle the game cards and place them faceup in a stack on the game board.
4. Have each player choose a castle tower.
5. Take turns choosing a game card from the pile and reading the words. If the words make a complete sentence, place the game card on your castle tower. If the words make a fragment, place the game card in the moat.
6. The first player to put five complete sentences in his castle tower is the winner.
7. Use the answer key to check your work.

Floating Fragments
Answer Key

Complete Sentences

Cara finished painting the fence.
The dog was thirsty.
Sharks are amazing animals.
May I have a cookie?
The cold, hungry cat wanted to come into the house.
The deer darted into the underbrush.
The lion growled loudly to warn the other lions.
The geese flew across the lake.
It is warm in here!
Would you please set the table for dinner?
You certainly didn't.

Fragments

My worst and best spelling scores.
On a long, hot, Saturday afternoon.
My summer vacation.
Sunny or rainy?
And broke off.
Ran as fast as she could.
If I could live in a castle.
A player from the other team.
A last, sad look at their house.

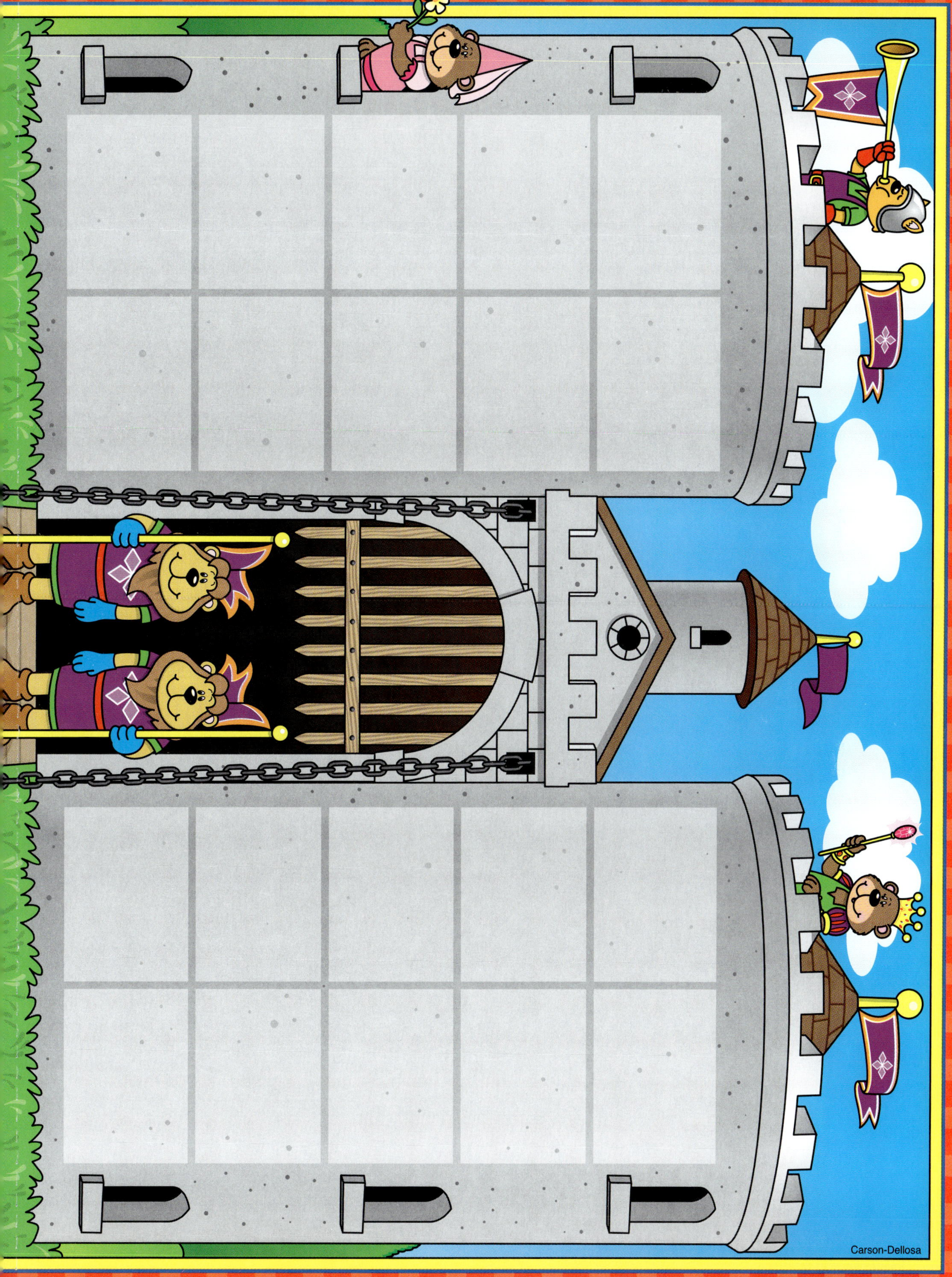
Carson-Dellosa

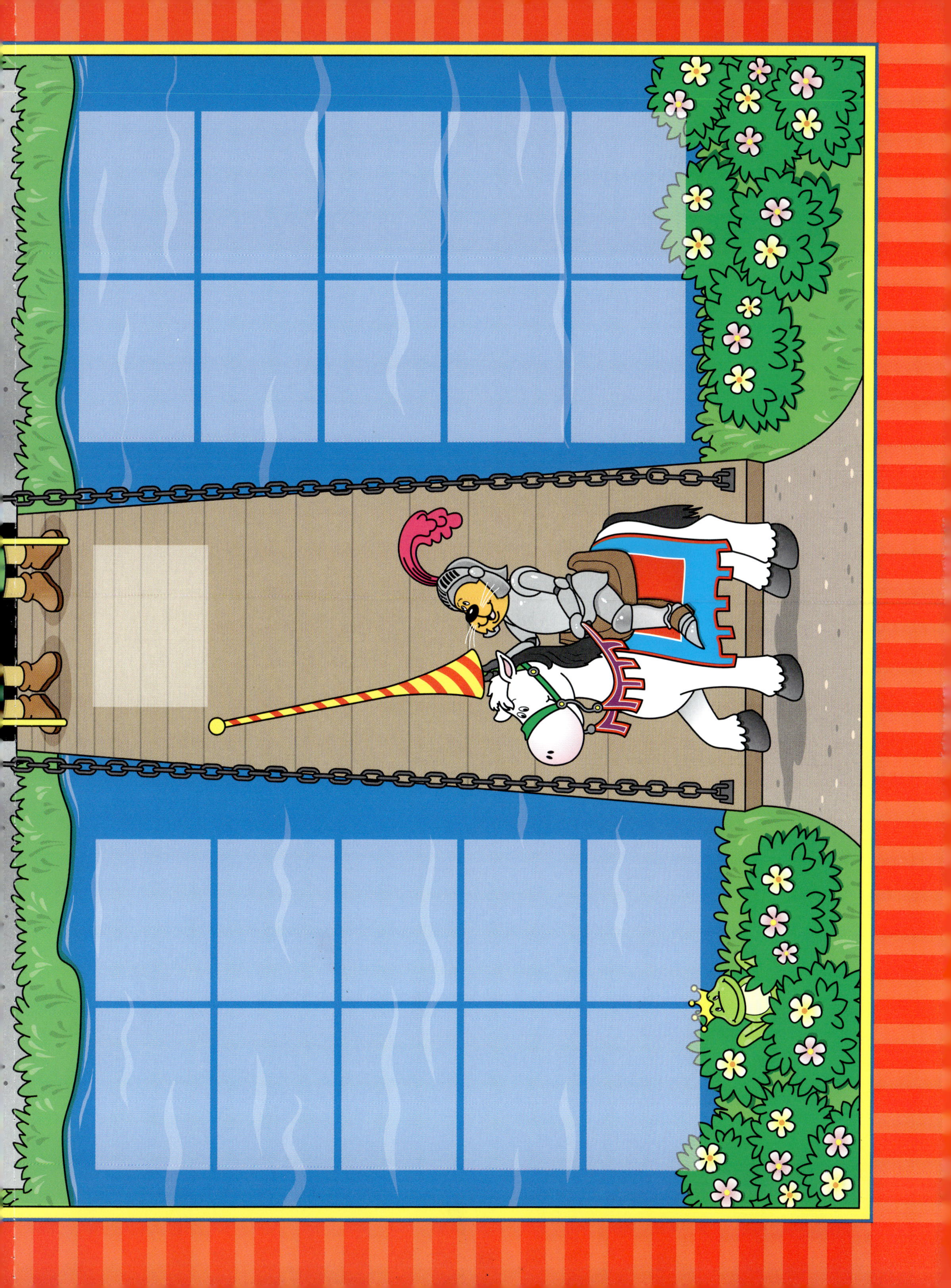

Floating Fragments

Cara finished painting the fence.	The deer darted into the underbrush.	My worst and best spelling scores.	Ran as fast she could.
The dog was thirsty.	The lion growled loudly to warn the other lions.	On a long, hot, Saturday afternoon.	If I could live in a castle.
Sharks are amazing animals.	The geese flew across the lake.	My summer vacation.	You certainly didn't.
May I have a cookie?	It is warm in here!	Sunny or rainy?	A player from the other team.
The cold, hungry cat wanted to come into the house.	Would you please set the table for dinner?	And broke off.	A last, sad look at their house.

Fishing for Facts

Directions

Game 1

1. Take the game cards and answer key out of the pocket. Set aside the starfish game cards. Place the fish game cards faceup around the game board.

2. Choose a game card and find the missing number to complete the problem.

3. Then, place the fish game card next to the bubble with the correct number.

4. Use the answer key to check your work.

Game 2

1. Take the game cards and answer key out of the pocket. Place the starfish game cards faceup around the game board.

2. Choose a bubble and read the number shown on it. Then, find a starfish game card with a number that is a multiple of the number shown on the bubble. Place the starfish game card on the bubble.

3. Continue playing until each bubble on the game board is covered by a starfish game card.

4. Use the answer key to check your work.

Fishing for Facts Answer Key

Game 1:

2 x (3) = 6
4 x (5) = 20
7 x (7) = 49
8 x (9) = 72
(4) x 3 = 12
(6) x 3 = 18
(8) x 3 = 24

6 x (4) = 24
8 x (6) = 48
4 x (8) = 32
(3) x 5 = 15
(5) x 8 = 40
(7) x 8 = 56
(9) x 2 = 18

27 ÷ 9 = (3)
45 ÷ 9 = (5)
63 ÷ 9 = (7)
81 ÷ 9 = (9)
36 ÷ (4) = 9
54 ÷ (6) = 9
72 ÷ (8) = 9

28 ÷ 7 = (4)
42 ÷ 7 = (6)
64 ÷ 8 = (8)
21 ÷ (3) = 7
35 ÷ (5) = 7
28 ÷ (7) = 4
90 ÷ (9) = 10

Game 2:

(3) 9, 12, 18, 24, 27
(4) 8, 12, 16, 24, 28, 32, 36
(5) 10, 25, 35, 40, 45
(6) 12, 18, 24, 36, 42, 48, 54
(7) 14, 28, 35, 42, 49, 56, 63
(8) 8, 16, 24, 32, 40, 48, 56, 72
(9) 9, 18, 27, 36, 45, 54, 63, 72, 81

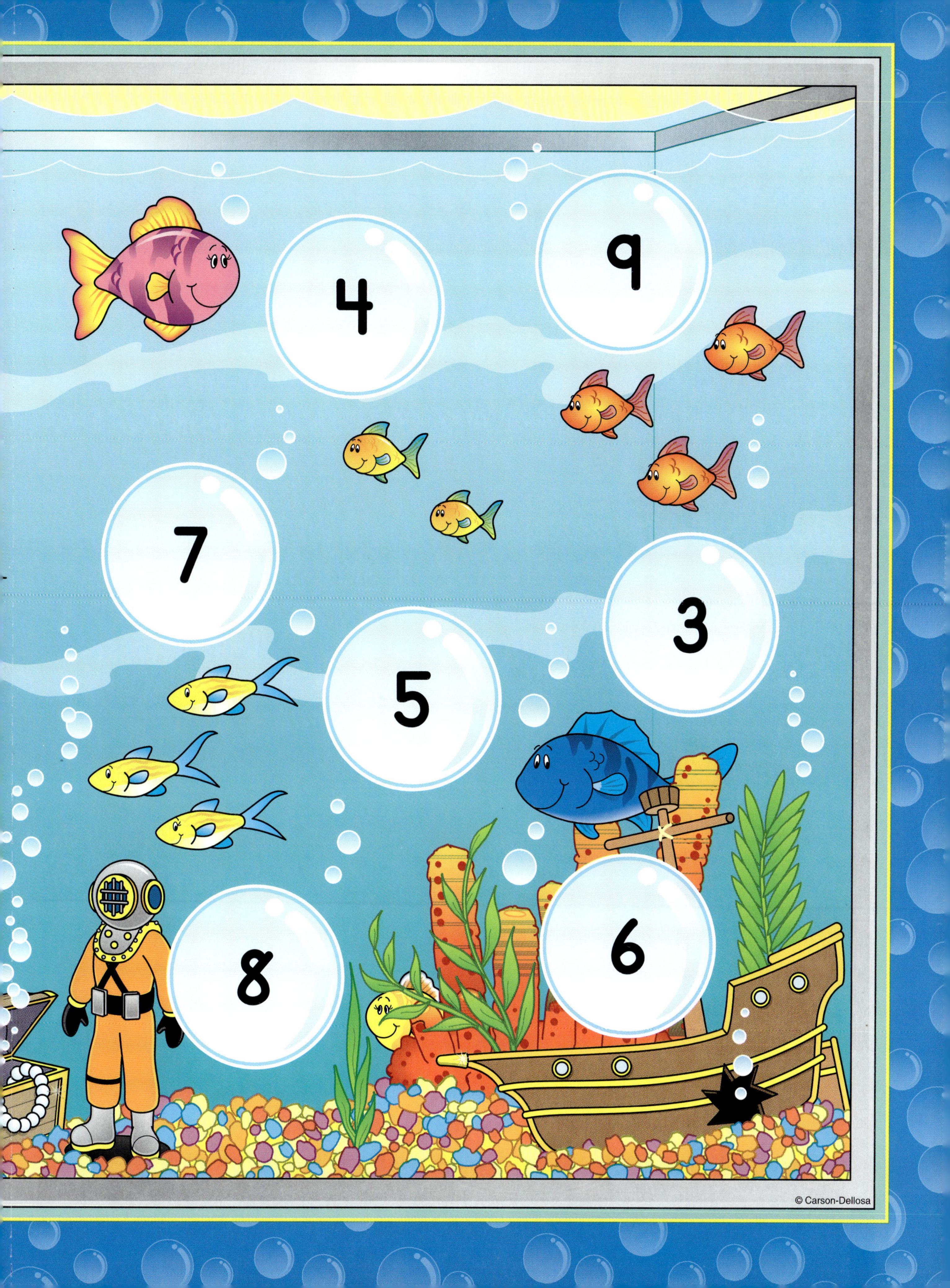
9
4
7
3
5
8
6

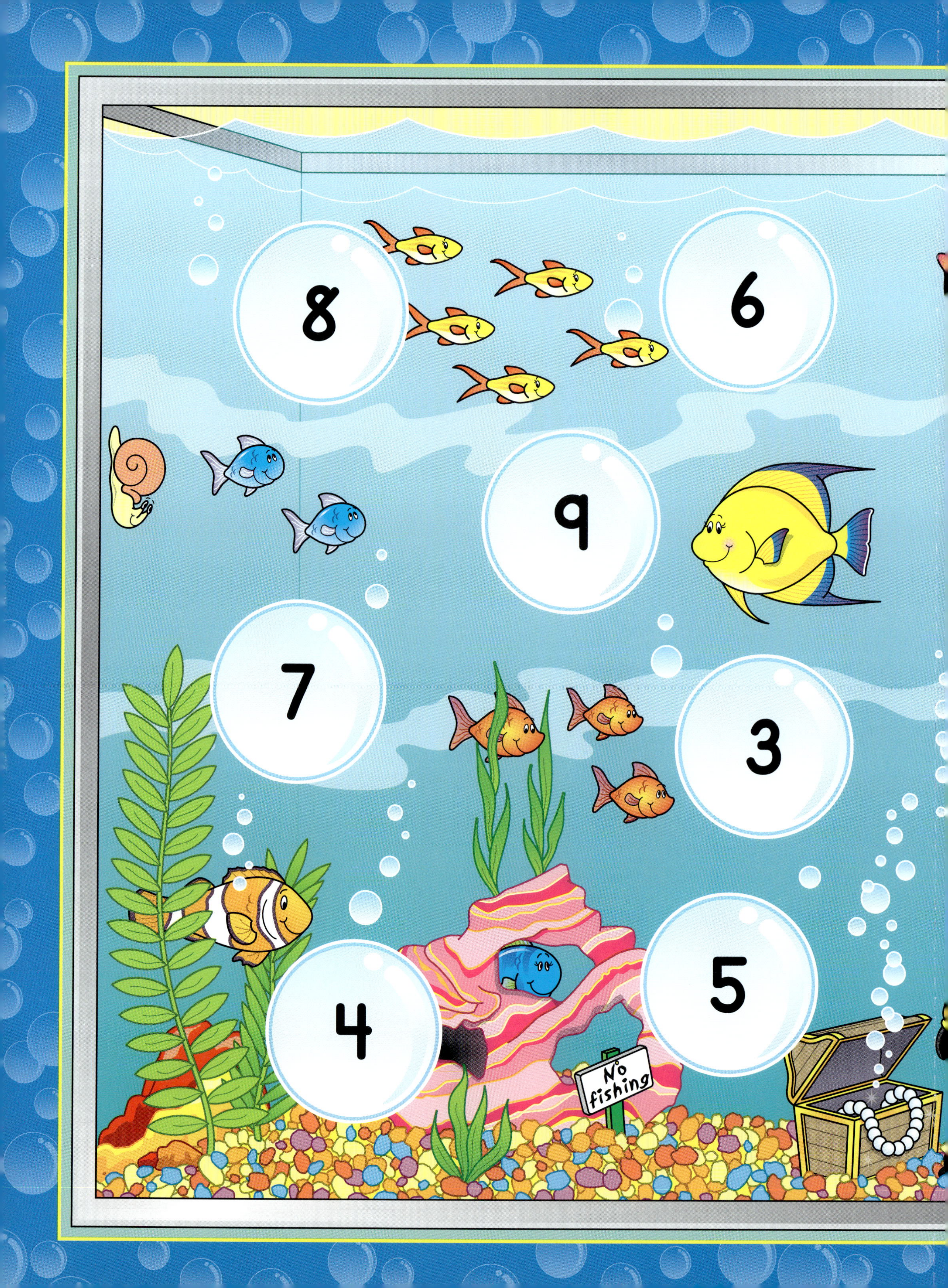
8
6
9
7
3
4
5
No fishing

Fishing for Facts

2 × __ = 6	__ × 5 = 15	27 ÷ 9 = __	21 ÷ __ = 7
6 × __ = 24	__ × 3 = 12	28 ÷ 7 = __	36 ÷ __ = 9
4 × __ = 20	__ × 8 = 40	45 ÷ 9 = __	35 ÷ __ = 7
8 × __ = 48	__ × 3 = 18	42 ÷ 7 = __	54 ÷ __ = 9
7 × __ = 49	__ × 8 = 56	63 ÷ 9 = __	28 ÷ __ = 4
4 × __ = 32	__ × 3 = 24	64 ÷ 8 = __	72 ÷ __ = 9
8 × __ = 72	__ × 2 = 18	81 ÷ 9 = __	90 ÷ __ = 10

Fishing for Facts

9	12	18	24
8	36	28	32
10	25	35	45
12	24	48	54
14	42	49	63
16	40	56	72
18	27	36	81

Planting Place Value

Directions

Game 1
1. Take the game cards and answer key out of the pocket. Set aside the yellow game cards. Place the blue game cards in a stack on the game board. Turn the answer key facedown.
2. Choose a game card and read the number. Decide whether the underlined number belongs in the ones, tens, hundreds, or thousands place.
3. Then, place the game card in the correct column on the game board.
4. Use the answer key to check your work.

Game 2
1. Set aside the game board.
2. Separate the yellow and blue game cards. Place the game cards faceup in two groups on a table or desktop.
3. Choose a yellow game card and read the problem shown. Then, find the blue game card that shows the answer to the problem. Place the matching game cards together.
4. Continue playing until all of the game cards have been matched.
5. Use the answer key to check your work.

Planting Place Value
Answer Key

Game 1:

thousands	hundreds	tens	ones
1,225	250	39	99
2,384	579	54	106
3,720	727	103	375
4,029	984	285	462
5,082	2,352	790	807
7,440	3,409	3,120	1,901
8,976	7,053	5,642	2,096
9,990	9,099	8,074	9,123

Game 2:

39 — 30 + 9
54 — 50 + 4
99 — 90 + 9
103 — 100 + 3
106 — 100 + 6
250 — 200 + 50
285 — 200 + 80 + 5
375 — 300 + 70 + 5
462 — 400 + 60 + 2
579 — 500 + 70 + 9
727 — 700 + 20 + 7
790 — 700 + 90
807 — 800 + 7
984 — 900 + 80 + 4
1,225 — 1,000 + 200 + 20 + 5
1,901 — 1,000 + 900 + 1

2,096 — 2,000 + 90 + 6
2,352 — 2,000 + 300 + 50 + 2
2,384 — 2,000 + 300 + 80 + 4
3,120 — 3,000 + 100 + 20
3,409 — 3,000 + 400 + 9
3,720 — 3,000 + 700 + 20
4,029 — 4,000 + 20 + 9
5,082 — 5,000 + 80 + 2
5,642 — 5,000 + 600 + 40 + 2
7,053 — 7,000 + 50 + 3
7,440 — 7,000 + 400 + 40
8,074 — 8,000 + 70 + 4
8,976 — 8,000 + 900 + 70 + 6
9,099 — 9,000 + 90 + 9
9,123 — 9,000 + 100 + 20 + 3
9,990 — 9,000 + 900 + 90

tens ones

hundreds

thousands

Planting Place Value

9_9_	_3_9	_2_50	_1_,225
10_6_	_5_4	_5_79	_2_,384
37_5_	1_0_3	_7_27	_3_,720
46_2_	2_8_5	_9_84	_4_,029
80_7_	7_9_0	2,_3_52	_5_,082
1,90_1_	3,1_2_0	3,_4_09	_7_,440
2,09_6_	5,6_4_2	7,_0_53	_8_,976
9,12_3_	8,0_7_4	9,_0_99	_9_,990

© Carson-Dellosa   49   CD-104051 *Colorful File Folder Games*

Planting Place Value

90 + 9	100 + 3	2,000 + 300 + 50 + 2
100 + 6	200 + 80 + 5	3,000 + 400 + 9
300 + 70 + 5	700 + 90	7,000 + 50 + 3
400 + 60 + 2	3,000 + 100 + 20	9,000 + 90 + 9
800 + 7	5,000 + 600 + 40 + 2	1,000 + 200 + 20 + 5
1,000 + 900 + 1	8,000 + 70 + 4	2,000 + 300 + 80 + 4
2,000 + 90 + 6	200 + 50	3,000 + 700 + 20
9,000 + 100 + 20 + 3	500 + 70 + 9	4,000 + 20 + 9
30 + 9	700 + 20 + 7	5,000 + 80 + 2
50 + 4	900 + 80 + 4	7,000 + 400 + 40
8,000 + 900 + 70 + 6	9,000 + 900 + 90	

Rounding Up Numbers

Directions

Game 1

1. Take the game cards and answer key out of the pocket. Set aside the blue game cards. Scatter the yellow game cards faceup around the game board. Turn the answer key facedown.

2. Look at the game board and choose a number. Round the number to the nearest 10. Find the answer on a yellow game card. Place the yellow game card on the number.

3. Continue playing until all of the numbers on the game board have been covered.

4. Use the answer key to check your work.

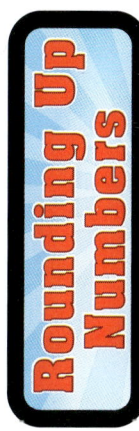

Game 2

1. Take the game cards and answer key out of the pocket. Set aside the yellow game cards. Scatter the blue game cards faceup around the game board. Turn the answer key facedown.

2. Look at the game board and choose a number. Round the number to the nearest 100. Find the answer on a blue game card. Place the blue game card on the number.

3. Continue playing until all of the numbers on the game board have been covered.

4. Use the answer key to check your work.

Rounding Up Numbers
Answer Key

Game 1: Nearest 10

	7,010	160	
1,040	320	410	2,690
840	6,710	1,570	350
7,090	970	940	7,180
	480	1,490	

Game 2: Nearest 100

	7,000	200	
1,000	300	400	2,700
800	6,700	1,600	400
7,100	1,000	900	7,200
	500	1,500	

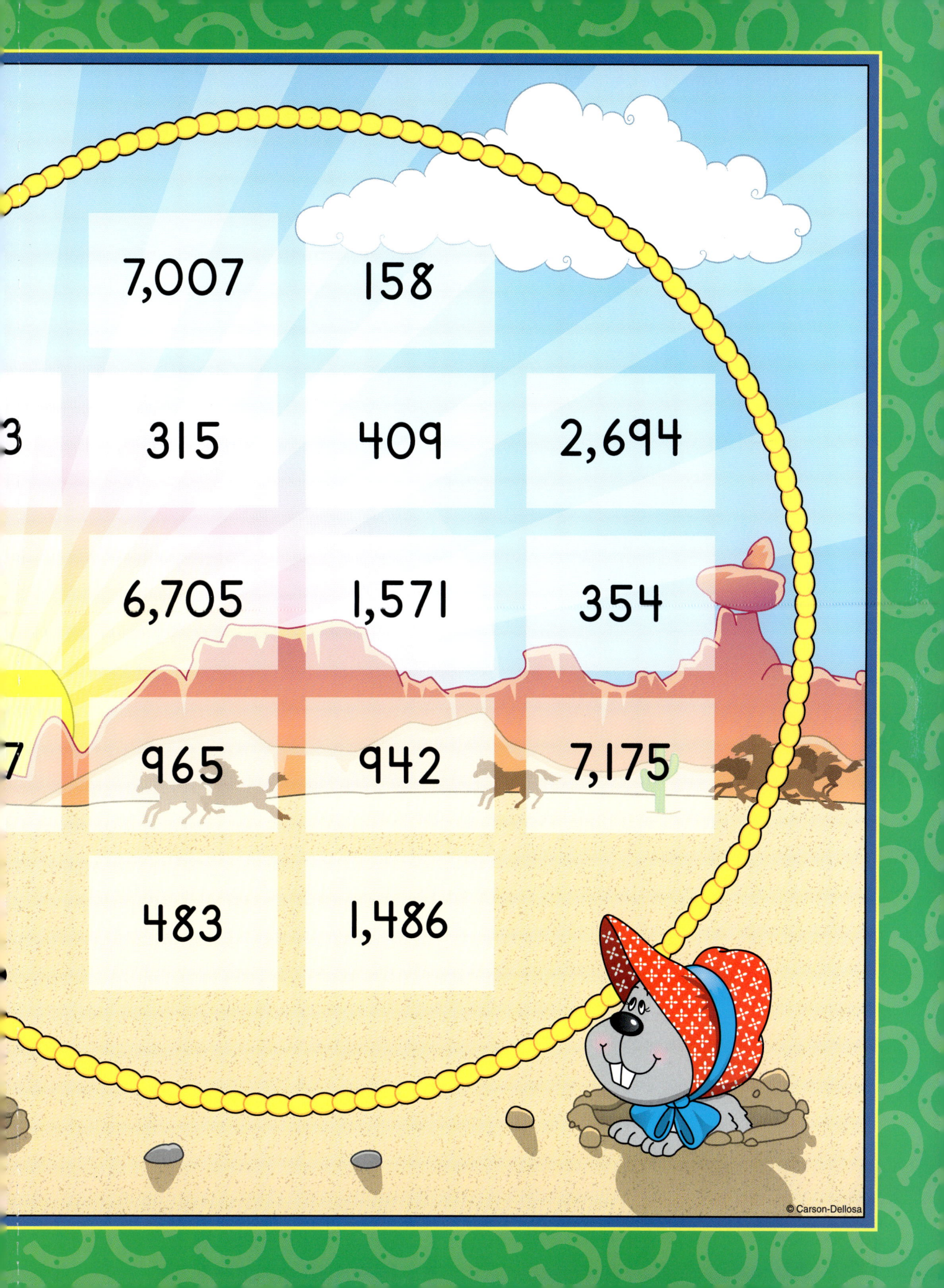

	7,007	158	
3	315	409	2,694
	6,705	1,571	354
7	965	942	7,175
	483	1,486	

7,087

837

1,043

Rounding Up Numbers

7,010	350	7,000	2,700
160	7,090	200	800
1,040	970	1,000	6,700
320	940	300	1,600
410	7,180	400	400
2,690	480	7,100	500
840	1,490	1,000	1,500
6,710	1,570	900	7,200

Directions

1. Ask a friend to play the game with you.

2. Take the game cards and answer key out of the pocket. Get a calculator, scrap paper, and a pencil for each player.

3. Sort the game cards by color. Place the game cards facedown in two stacks near the game board. Have each player choose a piggy bank on the game board.

4. Take turns choosing three game cards from each stack. Place the game cards faceup on your piggy bank.

5. Each player starts the game with $20.00 in her piggy bank.

6. Read all of the yellow game cards in your piggy bank. Add these amounts to your $20.00. Write the new total on your paper.

7. Then, read all of the orange game cards. Subtract these amounts from the total in your piggy bank. Write the new total on your paper.

8. The player with more money in her piggy bank after adding and subtracting is the winner.

9. Use a calculator to check your work.

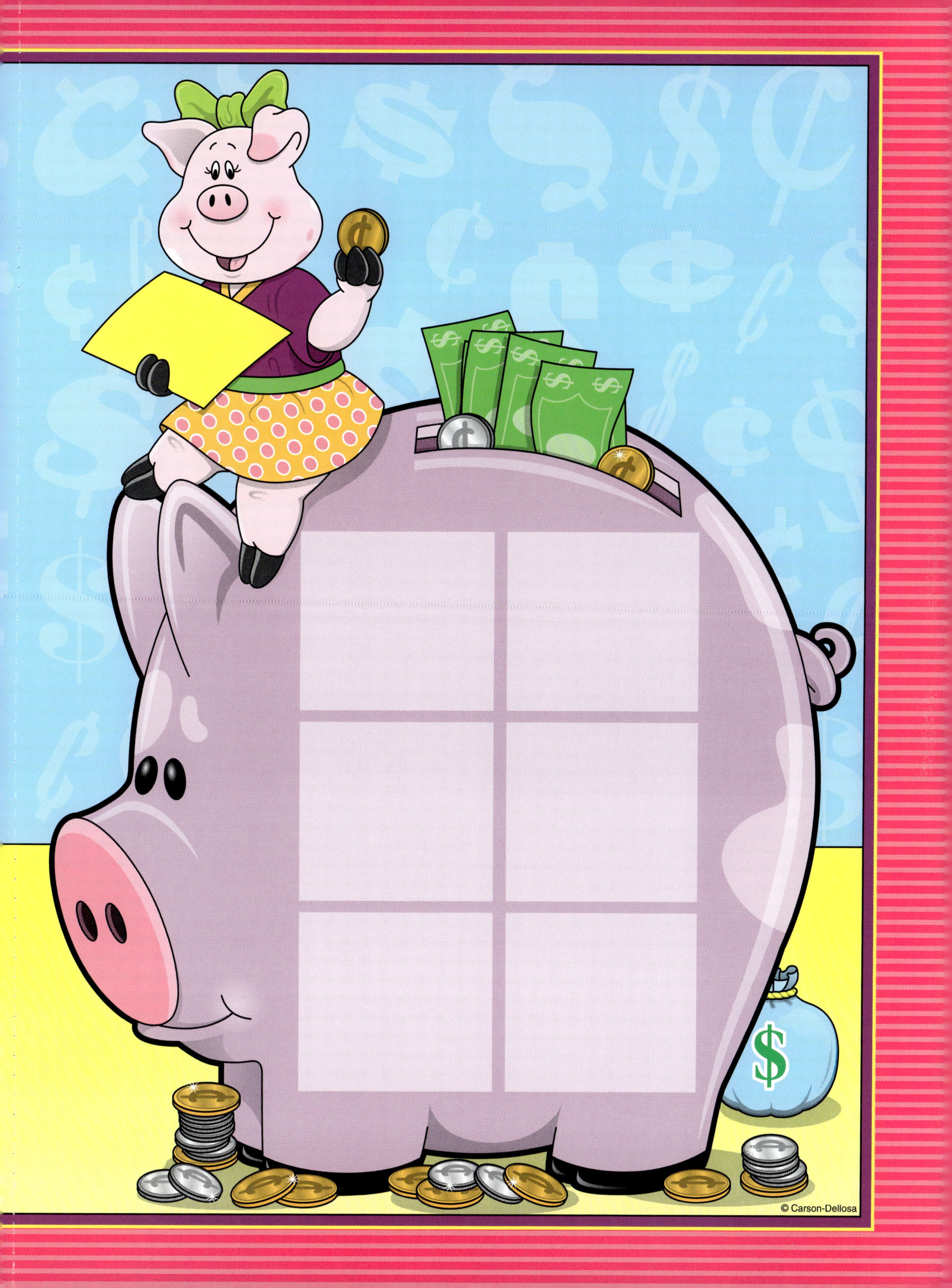

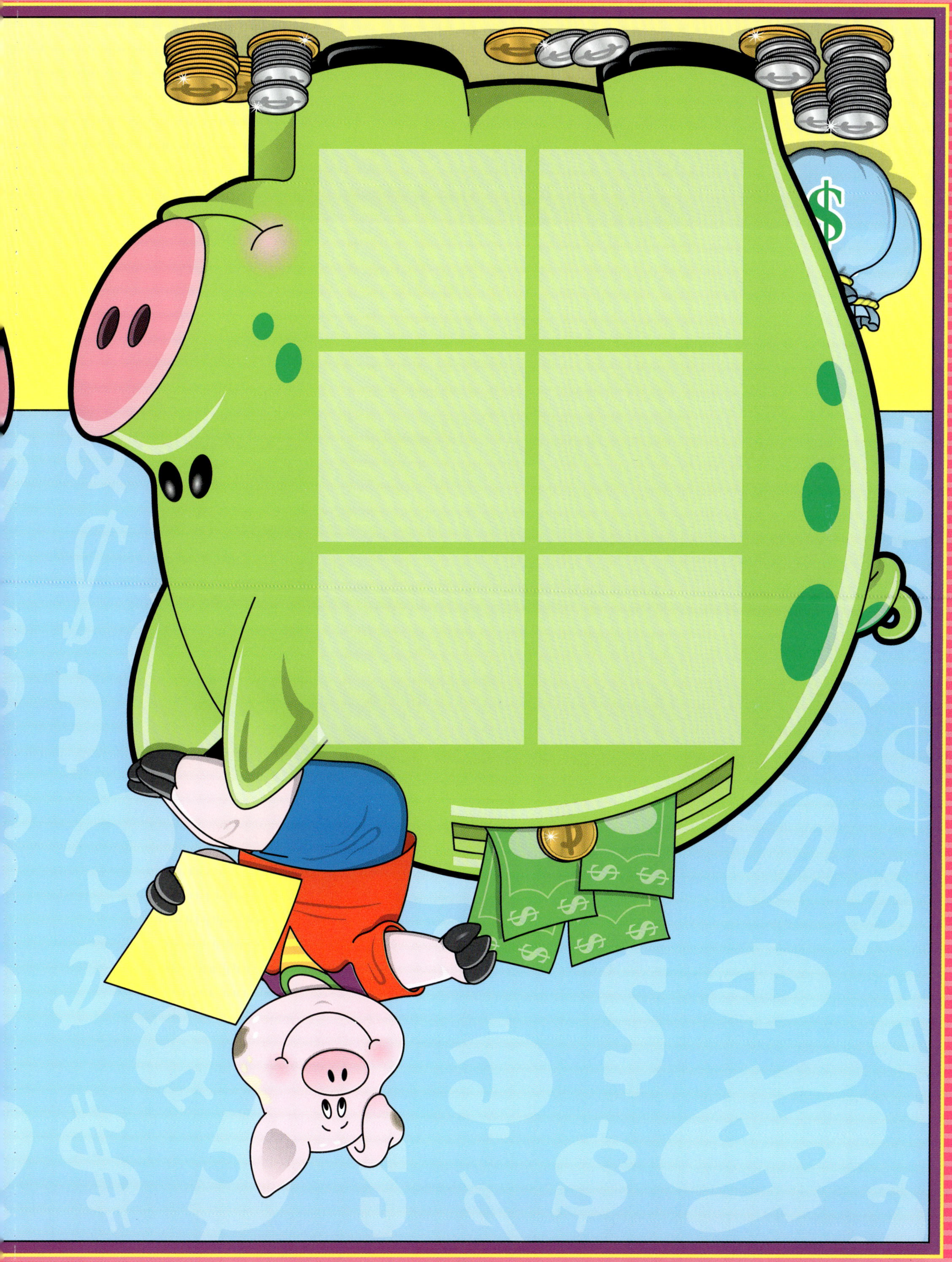

Making Money

You sell 5 glasses of lemonade at 25¢ each.	You earn $3.50 an hour by painting a fence. You work for 2 hours.	You sell your old bicycle for $16.50.	You sell some old toys for $11.00.
You sell your used in-line skates to a friend for $14.00.	You earn $3.00 an hour by raking leaves for your neighbor. You work for 2 hours.	You sell 8 glasses of lemonade for 25¢ each.	You sell 7 comic books from your collection for $1.00 each.
You earn $7.50 by planting flowers for your neighbor.	You earn $5.00 by taking care of your neighbor's dog.	You earn $12.00 by helping your grandparents move into a new house.	You earn $4.00 an hour by raking leaves. You work for 3 hours.
You receive $10.00 as a birthday gift.	You earn $8.00 by washing windows.	You buy a $3.00 collar for your puppy.	You buy a new book from the book fair. It costs $3.75.
You pay $1.50 for a soft pretzel at a baseball game.	You pay $2.50 for a hot dog and soda.	You pay $2.50 for a box of popcorn at the movies.	You pay $8.75 for a new T-shirt.
You pay $2.00 for a strawberry and vanilla ice-cream cone.	You spend $2.75 for a new erasable pen.	You buy a trading card that costs $5.00.	You buy a new soccer ball. It costs $10.00.

© Carson-Dellosa

CD-104051 *Colorful File Folder Games*

The Big Cheese

Directions

1. Ask a friend to play the game with you.

2. Take the game cards and game markers out of the pocket. Shuffle the game cards and place them facedown near the game board. Have each player choose a game marker. Then, each player should choose four game cards and place them faceup near the game board.

3. Look at your game cards and decide if any of the cards can be combined to equal one or more whole pizzas. If the cards equal one or more whole pizzas, you can move your game marker ahead the same number of spaces as whole pizzas made. Place the used game cards facedown in another pile near the game board. Then, choose more game cards from the stack to replace the discarded ones.

4. If one or more whole pizzas cannot be made by combining the game cards, choose another game card from the stack. Then, your friend can take a turn.

5. Continue playing until a player moves around the game board and lands on the big piece of cheese. The first player to reach the big piece of cheese is the winner.

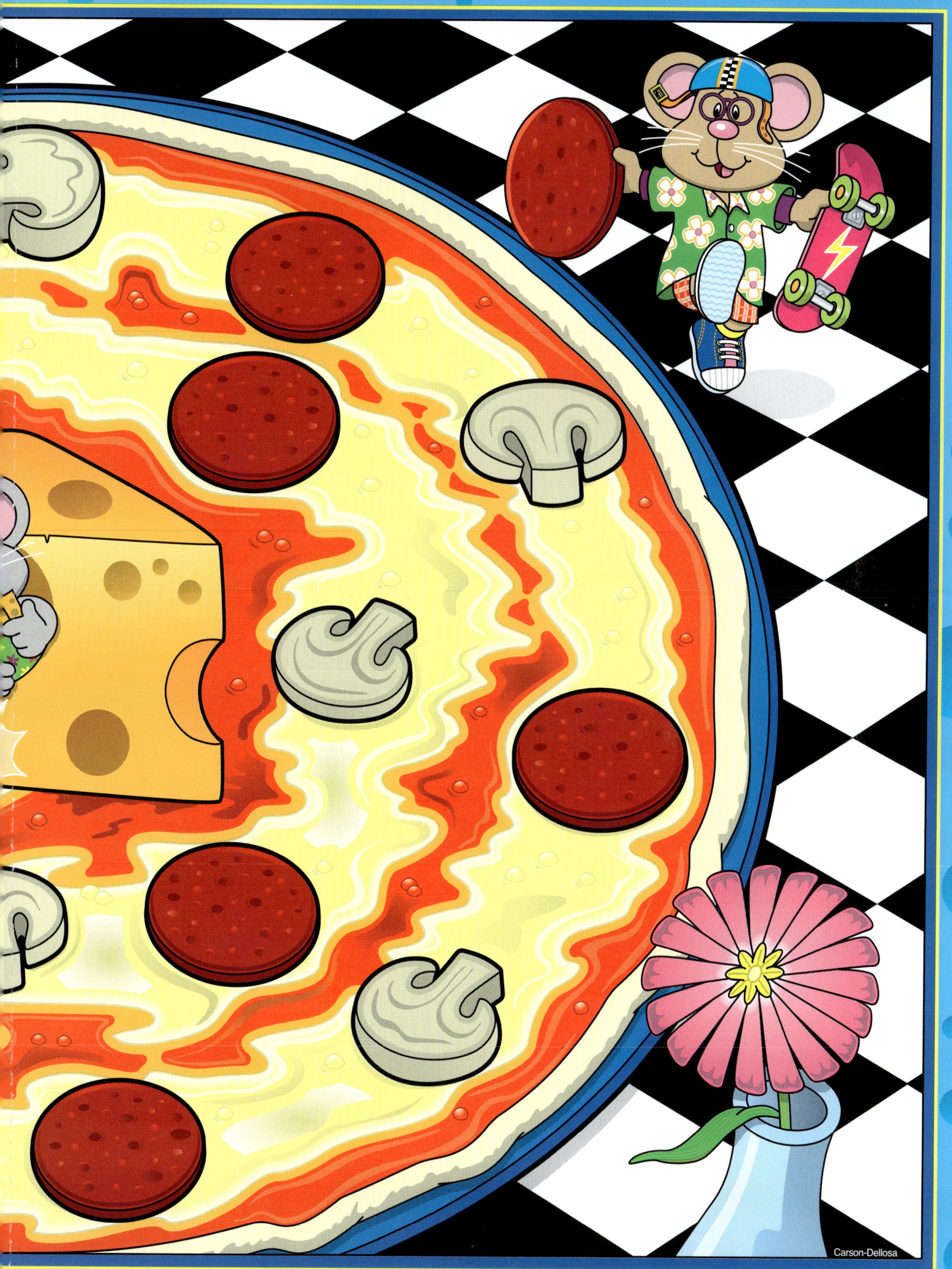
Carson-Dellosa

Finish

Start

I Love to Cook!

The Big Cheese

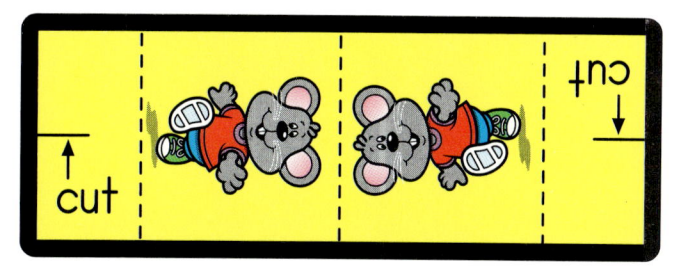

62

© Carson-Dellosa

CD-104051 *Colorful File Folder Games*

The Big Cheese

Measure Up!

Directions

Game 1

1. Ask a friend to play the game with you.
2. Take the picture cards, word cards, game markers, and answer key out of the pocket. Set aside the green word cards. Turn the answer key facedown.
3. Shuffle the picture cards and place them facedown in a stack on the game board. Then, shuffle the blue word cards and place them facedown in another stack on the game board.
4. Let each player choose eight picture cards and place them faceup near the game board.
5. Choose one blue word card, then decide if the unit of measurement shown can be used to measure an object shown on one of your picture cards. If a match is made, move your game marker the number of spaces shown in the hard hat on the blue word card. Use the answer key to check each other's work.
6. If a match cannot be made, return the blue word card to the bottom of the card pile. Then, your friend can take a turn.
7. The first player to reach the word "End" on the game board is the winner.

Game 2

Follow the directions for Game 1, using the green word cards instead of the blue word cards.

Measure Up! Answer Key

Games 1 & 2

	fluid ounce / milliliter		ounce / gram		mile / kilometer		inch / centimeter
	fluid ounce / milliliter		ounce / gram		mile / kilometer		inch / centimeter
	gallon / liter		pound / kilogram		ton / ton		yard / meter
	gallon / liter		pound / kilogram		ton / ton		yard / meter

© Carson-Dellosa

64

CD-104051 *Colorful File Folder Games*

Kit
6
7
8
9
10
11
12
13
14
15
16
17
18
19
20
21
Tool Kit
Crow Bar
Monkey Wrench

Start
1
2
3
4
5
Property of The Carpenter Ants
Builder Beaver
Hammerhead
End
22
23
24
25

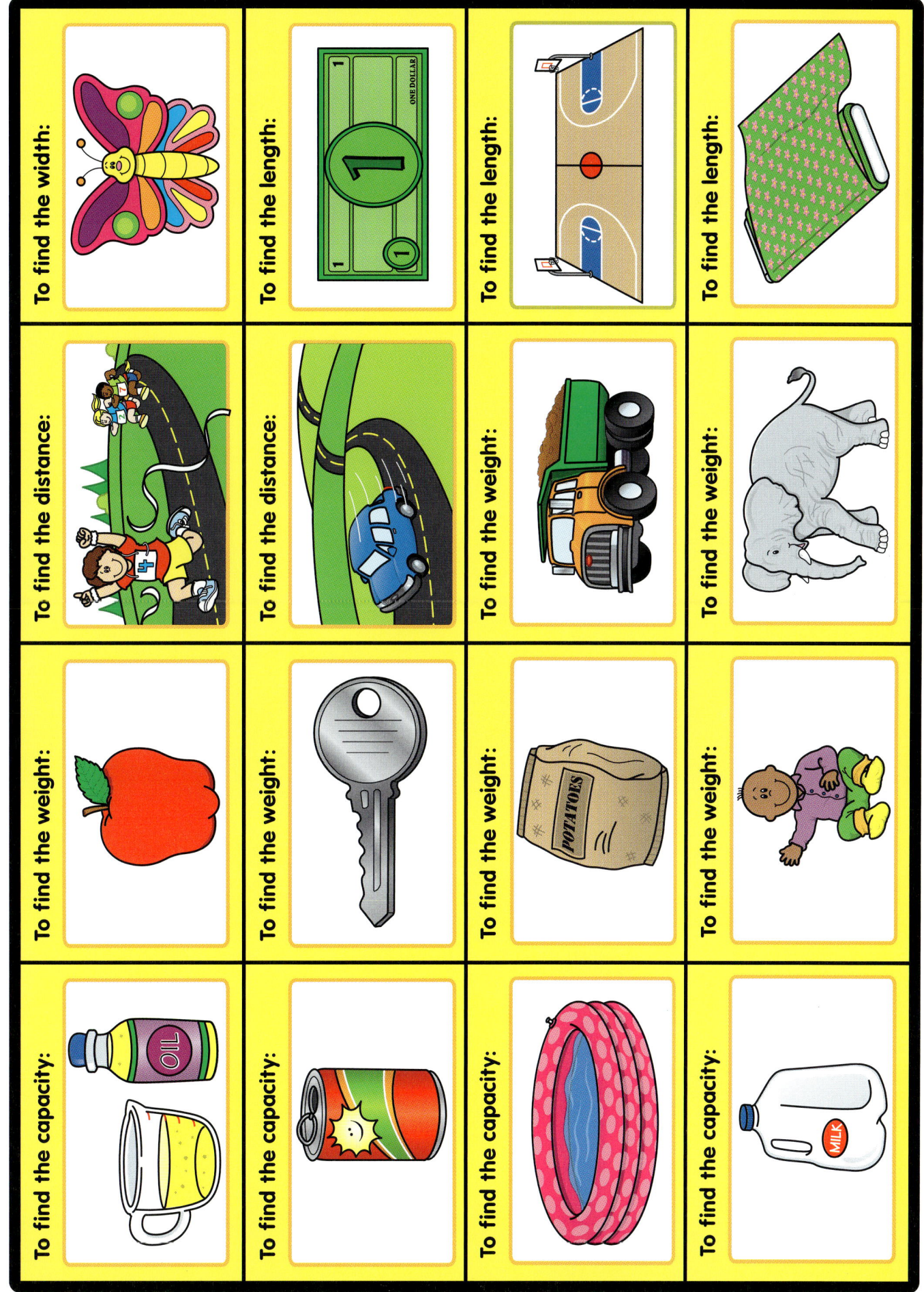

Measure Up!

To find the width:	To find the length:	To find the length:	To find the length:
To find the distance:	To find the distance:	To find the weight:	To find the weight:
To find the weight:	To find the weight:	To find the weight:	To find the weight:
To find the capacity:	To find the capacity:	To find the capacity:	To find the capacity:

© Carson-Dellosa 67 CD-104051 *Colorful File Folder Games*

Measure Up!

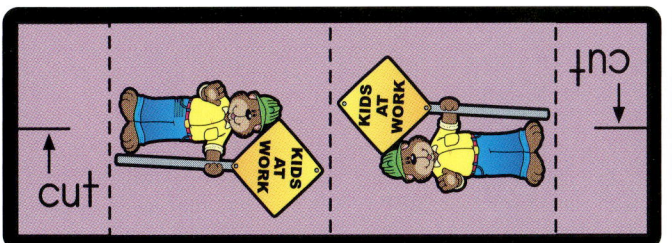

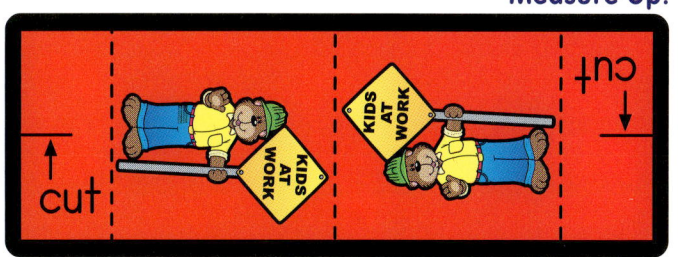

inch	3	kilometer	5	gram	3
inch	3	kilometer	5	gram	3
yard	4	meter	4	kilogram	4
yard	4	meter	4	kilogram	4
mile	5	centimeter	3	ton	5
mile	5	centimeter	3	ton	5
ounce	3	gallon	3	milliliter	2
ounce	3	gallon	3	milliliter	2
pound	4	fluid ounce	2	liter	3
pound	4	fluid ounce	2	liter	3
ton	5	ton	5	**Wild Card** Move ahead 5 spaces.	

Guessing Gum Balls

Directions

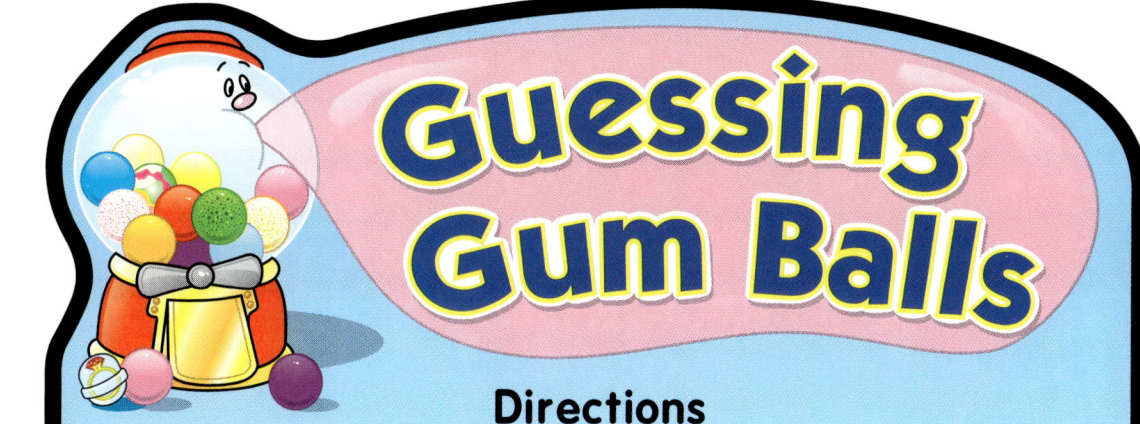

1. Ask a friend to play the game with you.
2. Take the game cards, gum balls, and answer key out of the pocket. Turn the answer key facedown.
3. Shuffle the game cards and place them facedown in a stack. Place the gum balls faceup near the game board. Let each player choose a gum ball machine on the game board.
4. Take turns drawing a game card and reading the problem. Then, find the gum ball on your gum ball machine that shows the fraction that answers the problem on your card.
5. Cover the fraction with a colorful gum ball that matches the color in your problem. If you cannot find the fraction on your gum ball machine, return the game card to the bottom of the stack.
6. Continue playing until one player covers all of the gum balls on his gum ball machine.
7. Use the answer key to check your work.
8. The first player to correctly cover all of the gum balls on his gum ball machine is the winner.

Guessing Gum Balls Answer Key

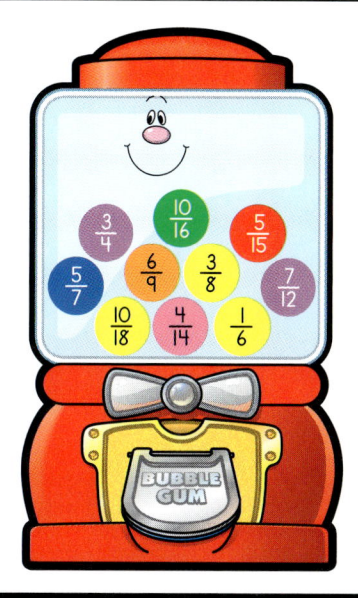

Machine 1: $\frac{13}{16}$, $\frac{5}{6}$, $\frac{7}{8}$, $\frac{8}{9}$, $\frac{11}{18}$, $\frac{3}{5}$, $\frac{3}{7}$, $\frac{5}{12}$, $\frac{3}{15}$, $\frac{2}{4}$

Machine 2: $\frac{3}{4}$, $\frac{10}{16}$, $\frac{5}{15}$, $\frac{5}{7}$, $\frac{6}{9}$, $\frac{3}{8}$, $\frac{7}{12}$, $\frac{10}{18}$, $\frac{4}{14}$, $\frac{1}{6}$

$\dfrac{3}{4}$　　$\dfrac{10}{16}$　　$\dfrac{5}{15}$

$\dfrac{5}{7}$　　$\dfrac{6}{9}$　　$\dfrac{3}{8}$　　$\dfrac{7}{12}$

$\dfrac{10}{18}$　　$\dfrac{4}{14}$　　$\dfrac{1}{6}$

$\frac{2}{5}$

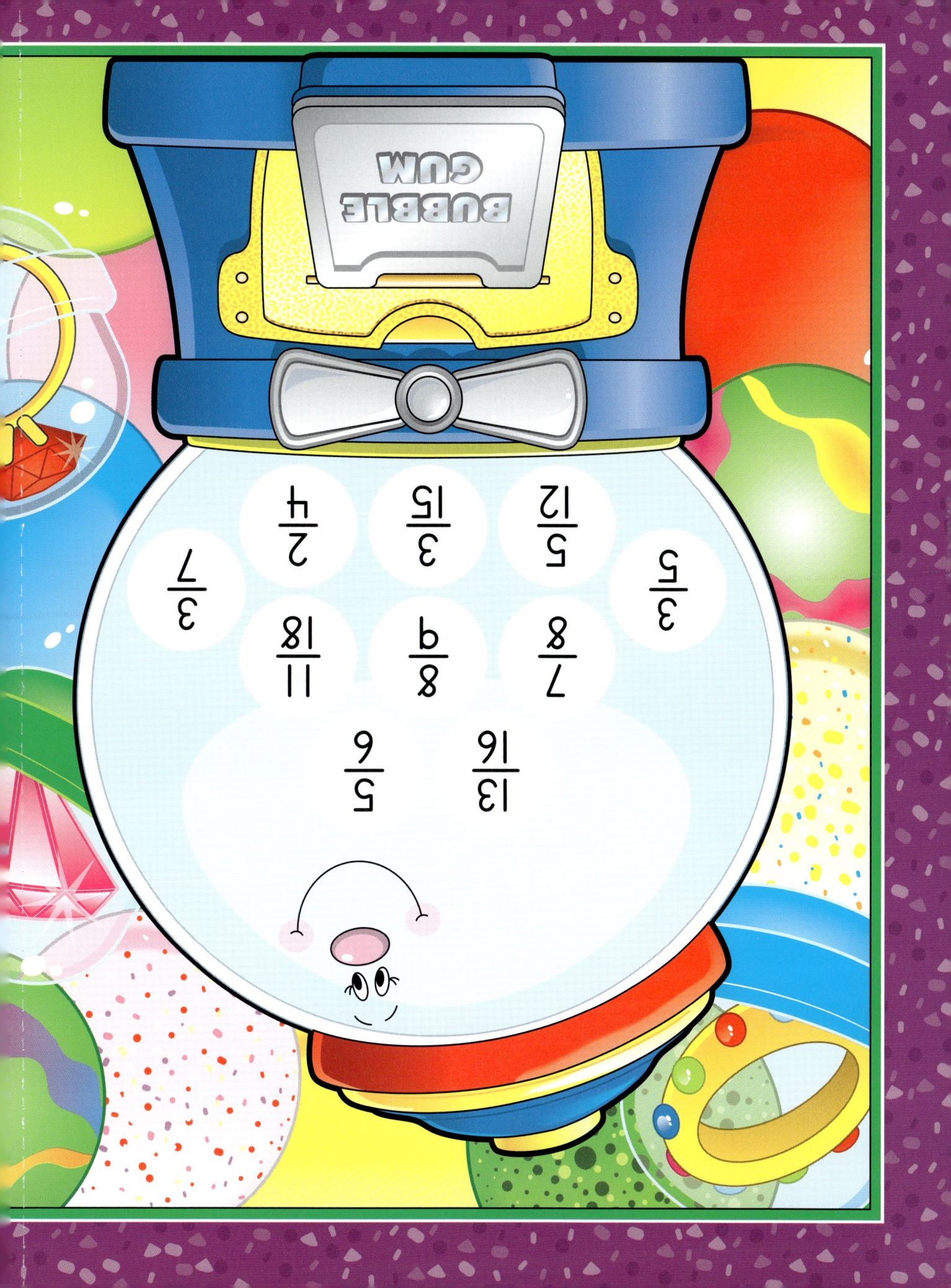

$\frac{3}{5}$ $\frac{15}{3}$ $\frac{12}{5}$

$\frac{7}{3}$ $\frac{4}{2}$ $\frac{8}{7}$

$\frac{11}{18}$ $\frac{9}{8}$ $\frac{16}{13}$

$\frac{5}{9}$

Guessing Gum Balls

What is the probability of getting a YELLOW gum ball?

What is the probability of getting an ORANGE gum ball?

What is the probability of getting a RED gum ball?

What is the probability of getting a BLUE gum ball?

What is the probability of getting a PURPLE gum ball?

What is the probability of getting a PINK gum ball?

What is the probability of getting a YELLOW gum ball?

What is the probability of getting an ORANGE gum ball?

What is the probability of getting a BLUE gum ball?

© Carson-Dellosa

CD-104051 *Colorful File Folder Games*

Guessing Gum Balls

What is the probability of getting a YELLOW gum ball?

What is the probability of getting an ORANGE gum ball?

What is the probability of getting a RED gum ball?

What is the probability of getting a BLUE gum ball?

What is the probability of getting a PURPLE gum ball?

What is the probability of getting a PINK gum ball?

What is the probability of getting a GREEN gum ball?

What is the probability of getting a GREEN gum ball?

What is the probability of getting a RED gum ball?

Guessing Gum Balls

What is the probability of getting a **YELLOW** gum ball?

What is the probability of getting a **GREEN** gum ball?

What's Cooking?

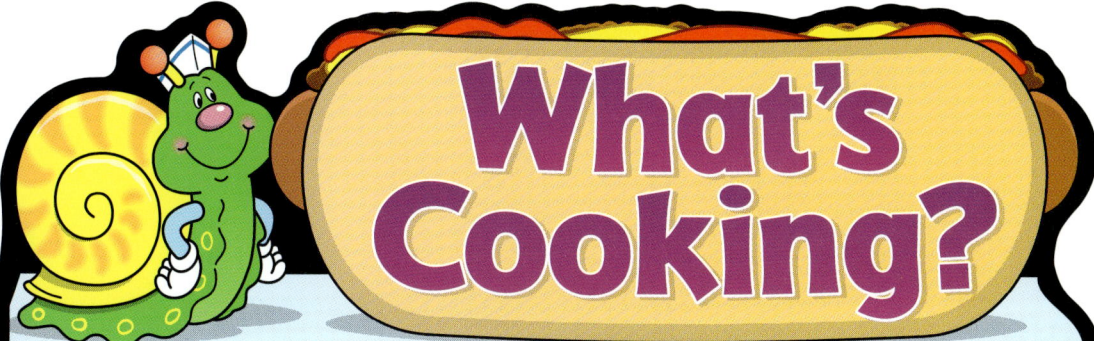

Directions

1. Ask a friend to play the game with you.

2. Take the game cards and plates out of the pocket.

3. Shuffle the game cards and place them facedown in a stack near the game board. Shuffle the plates and arrange them facedown around the game board. Have each player draw five plates.

4. Draw a game card and read the number of food orders on the card. Look at the numbers on plates you drew. Choose one plate that equals the order number in the game card. If needed, more than one plate can be added together to equal the order number on the game card. Place the plate or plates on the correct row on the game board to show the number of food orders on your game card. Then, place the game card in the purple box next to the food choice on the game board. Draw as many new plates as you placed on the game board.

5. If you do not have enough plates to equal the number on the game card, place the game card facedown at the bottom of the stack. Your friend may take a turn.

6. Continue playing until each food choice has 10 plates on the game board.

7. Check your work by adding the numbers on the game cards for each food choice. Then, add the numbers on the plates in that row. Those numbers should equal each other.

r of Orders

Place food orders here.

Key: ○ = 1 order

© Carson-Dellosa

Food Choices

Hot Dogs	
Tacos	
Burgers	
Salads	
Pizzas	

Number of

What's Cooking?

What's Cooking?

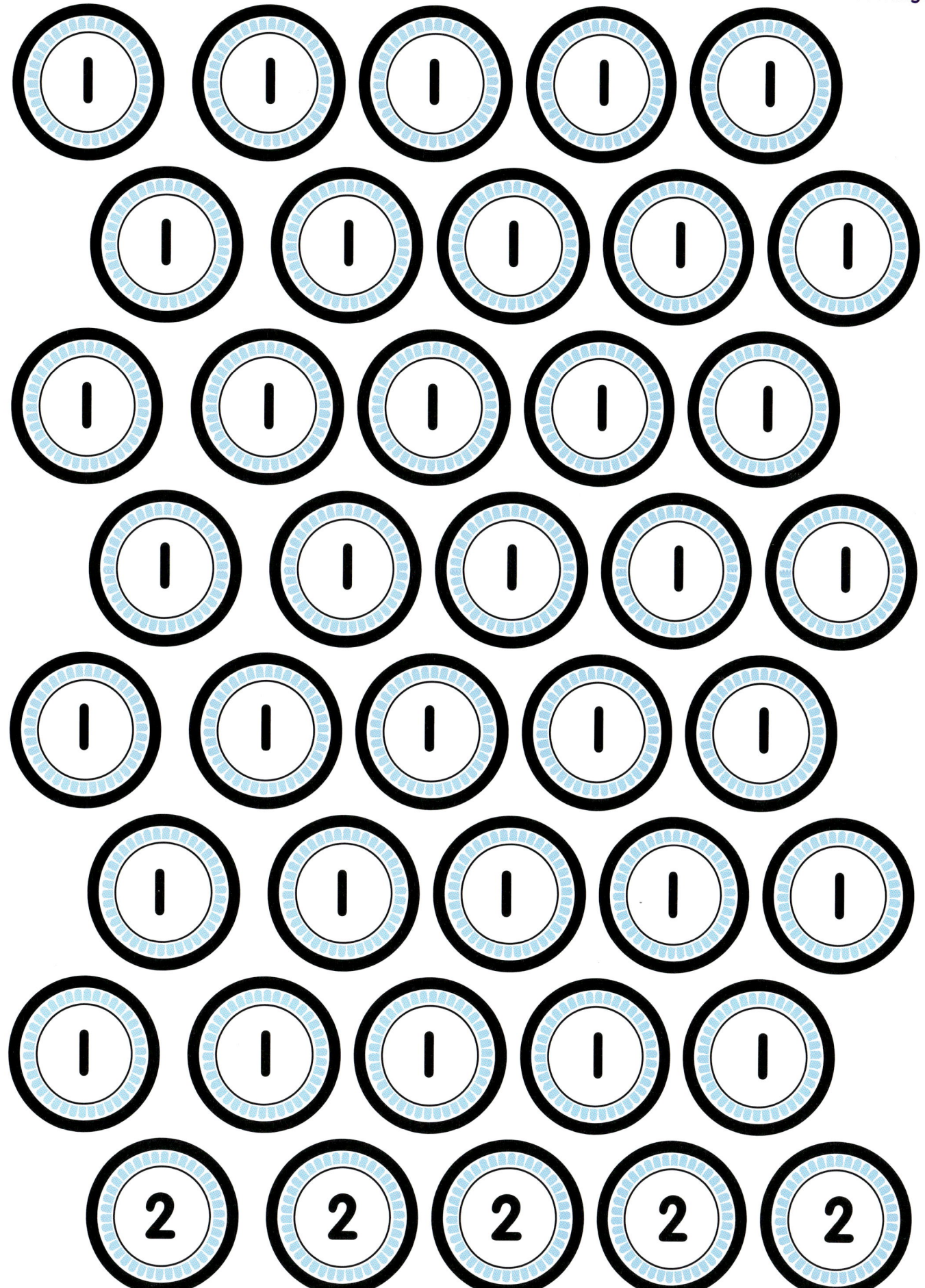

79

© Carson-Dellosa

CD-104051 *Colorful File Folder Games*

What's Cooking?

80

© Carson-Dellosa   CD-104051 *Colorful File Folder Games*